1001 Quotes for Great Leaders

Powerful Leadership Quotes for Inspiration, Motivation and Perspective

By Todd Hustel

Table of Contents

Introduction

"If I have seen further than others, it is by standing upon the shoulders of giants."

– Sir Isaac Newton, English physicist, mathematician, astronomer, alchemist, inventor, theologian and natural philosopher.

Thank you for choosing 1001 Quotes for Great Leaders: Powerful Leadership Quotes for Inspiration, Motivation and Perspective.

The journey to mastering leadership is long and has many steps. Whether you're just beginning your journey or you're a seasoned pro, this book has something for you.

The quotes in this book were collected throughout my professional lifetime and have been selected for this book from thousands of quotes in my library. You'll find useful quotes from ancient philosophers, clergyman, industrialists, political leaders and more.

Great leaders know they can find wisdom, inspiration and motivation from anywhere, anything, and they meet.

How to use this book

Leadership is a very broad topic. In order to make this book more useful and easier to read, the quotes in this book are separated into two sections. In the first section the quotes are separated into chapters based on an element of leadership. Each quote is listed alphabetically by the person's name in each chapter.

Section two provides a brief description of each person quoted and groups quotes by the individual. The people quoted are listed alphabetically by last name in this section, too.

At the very end of this text, you'll find an alphabetic listing of the people quoted in this book. Here you will see a listing of each page on which each individual quoted appears.

Here are three ways to use this book:
1. Browse the quotes at your leisure and appreciate their wisdom.
2. If you're seeking inspiration to address a specific issue, review a relevant section of this book for quotes from leaders that support the topic.
3. Use the index at the back of the book to find all the specific quotes contained in this book for each individual author.

Finally, I've made my best effort to trace the origin of each of these quotes. I was surprised by how many of the quotes are generally misattributed. If I've made an error, I will correct it in future editions of this book. I used no quotes with an anonymous source and omitted proverbs and quotes directly from religious texts.

If you are attributing quotes from this book, please reference the original author of the quote rather than only this book.

Enjoy 1001 Quotes for Great Leaders!

Section 1: Quotes by Topic

Chapter 1. Quotes About Leadership

Sure, there's a dictionary definition of leadership. This section is designed to enhance a basic definition of leadership by sharing quotes in which other leaders characterize what leadership is as well as what it is not. These quotes provide added color and practicality to the textbook definition. Read on...

If your actions inspire others to dream more, learn more, do more and become more, you are a leader. — John Quincy Adams

Try to be a rainbow in someone else's cloud. — Maya Angelou

Nothing can dim the light that shines from within. — Maya Angelou

He who cannot be a good follower cannot be a good leader. — Aristotle

The key to successful leadership is influence, not authority. — Roy T. Bennett

Leadership is the capacity to translate vision into reality. — Warren Bennis

The manager asks how and when; the leader asks what and why. — Warren Bennis

Good leaders make people feel that they're at the very heart of things, not at the periphery. — Warren Bennis

The art of leadership is saying no, not saying yes. It is very easy to say yes. — Tony Blair

Servant-leadership is all about making the goals clear and then rolling your sleeves up and doing whatever it takes to help people win. In that situation, they don't work for you, you work for them. — Ken Blanchard

Leadership is unlocking people's potential to become better. — Bill Bradley

The task of leadership is not to put greatness into humanity, but to elicit it, for the greatness is already there. — President James Buchanan

Effective leadership is putting first things first. Effective management is discipline, carrying it out. — Stephen Covey

The first responsibility of a leader is to define reality. The last is to say thank you. In between, the leader is a servant. — Max De Pree

Leaders don't inflict pain, they share pain. — Max De Pree

Leadership is much more an art, a belief, a condition of the heart, than a set of things to do. — Max De Pree

Leadership is liberating people to do what is required of them in the most effective and humane way possible. — Max De Pree

Above all, leadership is a position of servanthood. — Max De Pree

The greatest good you can do for another is not just to share your riches but to reveal to him his own. — Benjamin Disraeli

Great leaders harness personal courage, capture the hearts and minds of others and empower new leaders to make the world a better place. — Maxine Driscoll

Leadership is not magnetic personality, that can just as well be a glib tongue. It is not 'making friends and influencing people,' that is flattery. Leadership is lifting a person's vision to higher sights, the raising of a person's performance to a higher standard, the building of a personality beyond its normal limitations. — Peter F. Drucker

Leadership is lifting a person's vision to high sights, the raising of a person's performance to a higher standard, the building of a personality beyond its normal limitations. – Peter F. Drucker

The test of organization is not genius. It is its capacity to make common people achieve uncommon performance. — Peter F. Drucker

Management is doing the right thing; leadership is doing the right things. — Peter F. Drucker

It is the capacity to develop and improve their skills that distinguishes leaders from followers. — Peter F. Drucker

Effective leadership is not about making speeches or being liked; leadership is defined by results, not attributes. — Peter F. Drucker

You do not lead by hitting people over the head - that's assault, not leadership. — President Dwight D. Eisenhower

Pull the string, and it will follow wherever you wish. Push it, and it will go nowhere at all. — President Dwight D. Eisenhower

Always try to associate yourself with and learn as much as you can from those who know more than you do, who do better than you, who see more clearly than you. — President Dwight D. Eisenhower

In most cases being a good boss means hiring talented people and then getting out of their way. — Tina Fey

Inspiring conduct has so much more of an impact than coercing it. — Thomas Friedman

All of the great leaders have had one characteristic in common: it was the willingness to confront unequivocally the major anxiety of their people in their time. This, and not much else, is the essence of leadership. — John Kenneth Galbraith

I suppose leadership at one time meant muscles; but today it means getting along with people. — Mahatma Gandhi

Leadership cannot really be taught. It can only be learned. — Harold Geneen

Look over your shoulder now and then to be sure someone's following you. — Henry Gilmer

One of the tests of leadership is the ability to recognize a problem before it becomes an emergency. — Arnold Glasow

A good leader takes a little more than his share of the blame, a little less than his share of the credit. — Arnold Glasow

Leadership is the art of giving people a platform for spreading ideas that work. — Seth Godin

The secret of leadership is simple: Do what you believe in. Paint a picture of the future. Go there. People will follow. — Seth Godin

Leadership, on the other hand, is about creating change you believe in. — Seth Godin

The most effective leaders aren't extraverts or introverts. They're ambiverts: people who strike a balance of talking and listening. — Adam Grant

Two commanders on the same field are always one too many. — President Ulysses S. Grant

Control is not leadership; management is not leadership; leadership is leadership. If you seek to lead, invest at least 50 percent of your time in leading yourself--your own purpose, ethics, principles, motivation, conduct. Invest at least 20 percent leading those with authority over you and 15 percent leading your peers. — Dee Hock

Earn your leadership every day. — Michael Jordan

Leadership is an ever-evolving position. — Mike Krzyzewski

It is better to lead from behind and to put others in front, especially when you celebrate victory when nice things occur. You take the front line when there is danger. Then people will appreciate your leadership. — Nelson Mandela

He who wishes to be obeyed must know how to command. — Niccolò Machiavelli

A good leader is a person who takes a little more than his share of the blame and a little less than his share of the credit. — John C. Maxwell

Leadership is an action, not a position. — Donald McGannon

To do great things is difficult; but to command great things is more difficult. — Friedrich Nietzsche

True leadership lies in guiding others to success--in ensuring that everyone is performing at their best, doing the work they are pledged to do and doing it well. — Bill Owens

Be willing to make decisions. That's the most important quality in a good leader — General George S. Patton

Servant-leadership is more than a concept, it is a fact. Any great leader, by which I also mean an ethical leader of any group, will see herself or himself as a servant of that group and will act accordingly. — M. Scott Peck

Leadership is solving problems. The day soldiers stop bringing you their problems is the day you have stopped leading them. They have either lost confidence that you can help or concluded you do not care. Either case is a failure of leadership. — General Colin Powell

What great leaders have in common is that each truly knows his or her strengths - and can call on the right strength at the right time. — Tom Rath

You cannot be a leader, and ask other people to follow you, unless you know how to follow, too. — Sam Rayburn

The greatest leader is not necessarily the one who does the greatest things. He is the one that gets the people to do the greatest things. — President Ronald Reagan

The challenge of leadership is to be strong, but not rude; be kind, but not weak; be bold, but not bully; be thoughtful, but not lazy; be humble, but not timid; be proud, but not arrogant; have humor, but without folly. — Jim Rohn

To handle yourself, use your head; to handle others, use your heart. — Eleanor Roosevelt

Leadership is about making others better as a result of your presence and making sure that impact lasts in your absence. — Sheryl Sandberg

Leadership is not about a title or a designation. It's about impact, influence, and inspiration. — Robin S. Sharma

A star wants to see himself rise to the top. A leader wants to see those around him rise to the top. — Simon Sinek

Leadership is a series of behaviors rather than a role for heroes. — Margaret J. Wheatley

Leadership requires belief in the mission and unyielding perseverance to achieve victory. — Jocko Willink

Great leaders are not defined by the absence of weakness, but rather by the presence of clear strengths. — John Zenger

Chapter 2: Quotes About What Leaders Do

While researching this book it became clear to me that there was a difference between quotes about leadership and quotes about what leaders do. In the section of the book you'll find quotes from leaders around the globe and throughout time in history that help describe what a leader does.

A good leader leads the people from above them. A great leader leads the people from within them. — M. D. Arnold

A leader is a person you will follow to a place you would not go by yourself. — Joel Barker

Becoming a leader is synonymous with becoming yourself. It is precisely that simple and it is also that difficult. — Warren Bennis

Leaders are people who believe so passionately that they can seduce other people into sharing their dream. — Warren Bennis

A leader is a dealer in hope. — Napoléon Bonaparte

A leader is someone who holds her- or himself accountable for finding the potential in people and processes. — Brené Brown

A hero is someone who has given his or her life to something bigger than oneself. — Joseph Campbell

No man will make a great leader who wants to do it all himself or get all the credit for doing it. — Andrew Carnegie

A leader takes people where they want to go. A great leader takes people where they don't necessarily want to go, but ought to be. — Rosalynn Carter

Leaders come in two flavors, expanders and containers. The best leadership teams have a mix of both. — Barbara Corcoran

The leader is the servant who removes the obstacles that prevent people from doing their jobs. — Max De Pree

Leaders don't inflict pain, they share pain. — Max De Pree

Leadership is like third grade: it means repeating the significant things. — Max De Pree

True leaders understand that leadership is not about them but about those they serve. It is not about exalting themselves but about lifting others up. — Sheri Dew

Wise leaders generally have wise counselors because it takes a wise person themselves to distinguish them. — Diogenes of Sinope

I must follow the people. Am I not their leader? — Prime Minister Benjamin Disraeli

Your first and foremost job as a leader is to take charge of your own energy and then help to orchestrate the energy of those around you. — Peter F. Drucker

A leader is one who sees more than others see, who sees farther than others see, and who sees before others see. — Leroy Eimes

Ninety percent of leadership is the ability to communicate something people want. — Senator Dianne Feinstein

The growth and development of people is the highest calling of leadership — Harvey S. Firestone

Leaders need to provide strategy and direction and to give employees the tools that enable them to gather information and insight from around the world. Leaders shouldn't try to make every decision. — Bill Gates

As we look ahead into the next century, leaders will be those who empower others. — Bill Gates

The highest of distinctions is service to others. — King George VI

The role of leadership is to transform the complex situation into small pieces and prioritize them. — Carlos Ghosn

How was your day? If your answer was "fine," then I don't think you were leading. — Seth Godin

In a battle between two ideas, the best one doesn't necessarily win. No, the idea that wins is the one with the most fearless heretic behind it. — Seth Godin

There is something more scarce, something rarer than ability. It is the ability to recognize ability. — Robert Half

The greatest ability in business is to get along with others and influence their actions. — John Hancock

Real leadership is leaders recognizing that they serve the people that they lead. — Pete Hoekstra

You manage things; you lead people. — Rear Admiral Grace Hopper

The art of communication is the language of leadership. — James Humes

My job is not to be easy on people. My job is to take these great people we have and to push them and make them even better. — Steve Jobs

A genuine leader is not a searcher for consensus, but a molder of consensus. — Dr. Martin Luther King Jr.

The task of the leader is to get their people from where they are to where they have not been. — Henry Kissinger

Leaders aren't born, they are made. And they are made just like anything else, through hard work. And that's the price we'll have to pay to achieve that goal, or any goal — Vince Lombardi

A leader should have higher grit and tenacity and be able to endure what the employees can't. — Jack Ma

It is not titles that honour men, but men that honour titles. — Niccolò Machiavelli

If you want to lead on the highest level, be willing to serve on the lowest. — John C. Maxwell

Always remember, Son, the best boss is the one who bosses the least. Whether it's cattle, or horses, or men; the least government is the best government. — Ralph Moody

The function of leaders is to produce more leaders, not more followers. — Ralph Nader

My job as a leader is to make sure everybody in the company has great opportunities, and that they feel they're having a meaningful impact. — Larry Page

If your actions create a legacy that inspires others to dream more, learn more, do more and become more, then, you are an excellent leader. — Dolly Parton

Human behavior flows from three main sources: desire, emotion, and knowledge. — Plato

Great leaders are almost always great simplifiers, who can cut through argument, debate, and doubt to offer a solution everybody can understand. — General Colin Powell

Don't blame the marketing department. The buck stops with the chief executive. — John D. Rockefeller

A good objective of leadership is to help those who are doing poorly to do well and to help those who are doing well to do even better. — Jim Rohn

People ask the difference between a leader and a boss. The leader leads, and the boss drives. — President Theodore Roosevelt

The test of leadership is, is anything or anyone better because of you? — Mark Sanborn

I don't know what your destiny will be, but one thing I know: The only ones among you who will be truly happy are those who have sought and found how to serve. — Albert Schweitzer

A boss has the title, a leader has the people. — Simon Sinek

The leaders who get the most out of their people are the leaders who care most about their people. — Simon Sinek

People who enjoy meetings should not be in charge of anything. — Thomas Sowell

A leader is not an administrator who loves to run others, but someone who carries water for his people so that they can get on with their jobs. — Robert Townsend

Become the kind of leader that other people would follow voluntarily; even if you had no title or position. — Brian Tracy

Leaders think and talk about the solutions. Followers think and talk about the problems. — Brian Tracy

Leaders, true leaders, take responsibility for the success of the team, and understand that they must also take responsibility for the failure. — President Donald J. Trump

A great person attracts great people and knows how to hold them together. — Johann Wolfgang von Goethe

Require nothing unreasonable of your officers and men but see that whatever is required be punctually complied with. Reward and punish every man according to his merit, without partiality or prejudice; hear his complaints; if well founded, redress them; if otherwise, discourage them, in order to prevent frivolous ones. Discourage vice in every shape, and impress upon the mind of every man, from the first to the lowest, the importance of the cause, and what it is they are contending for. — President George Washington

People have to trust you. You have to build in trust for people. — Jack Welch

Leading people is the most challenging and, therefore, the most gratifying undertaking of all human endeavors. — Jocko Willink

I not only use all the brains that I have, but all that I can borrow. — President Woodrow Wilson

One cool judgment is worth a thousand hasty counsels. The thing to do is to supply light and not heat. — President Woodrow Wilson

A coach is someone who can give correction without causing resentment. — John Wooden

Chapter 3: Quotes about Vision

One critical tasks of leaders is to share their vision. Vision applies to the organization and to the task at hand. It must be communicated to the people in their charge in a way that is compelling and actionable. The quotes in this section offer a collection of ideas and thoughts about how leaders cast vision across the organization.

The bad news is time flies. The good news is you're the pilot. — Michael Altshuler

If you don't set goals, you can't regret not reaching them. — Yogi Berra

The greatest leaders mobilize others by coalescing people around a shared vision. — Ken Blanchard

Connect the dots between individual roles and the goals of the organization. When people see that connection, they get a lot of energy out of work. They feel the importance, dignity, and meaning in their job. — Ken Blanchard

Envisioning the end is enough to put the means in motion. — Dorthea Brande

Go as far as you can see; when you get there, you'll be able to go further. — Thomas Carlisle

The lightning spark of thought generated in the solitary mind awakens its likeness in another mind. — Thomas Carlisle

There is only one thing that makes a dream impossible to achieve: the fear of failure. — Paul Coelho

Having a vision for what you want is not enough. Vision without execution is hallucination. — Thomas A. Edison

It isn't where you came from. It's where you're going that counts. — Ella Fitzgerald

You must be the change you wish to see in the world. — Mahatma Gandhi

The vision is really about empowering workers, giving them all the information about what's going on so they can do a lot more than they've done in the past. — Bill Gates

Forget about trying to compete with someone else. Create your own pathway. Create your own new vision. — Herbie Hancock

The very essence of leadership is that you have to have vision. You can't blow an uncertain trumpet. — Father Theodore M. Hesburgh

The great thing in this world is not so much where you stand, as in what direction you're moving. — Oliver Wendell Holmes

Vision attracts resources. — Michael Hyatt

We need only in cold blood act as if the thing in question were real and it will. Become infallibly real. By growing into such a connection with our life that it will become real. It will become so knit with habit and emotion that our interests in it will be those which characterize belief. — William James

Yesterday is not ours to recover, but tomorrow is ours to win or to lose. — President Lyndon B. Johnson

A leader has the vision and conviction that a dream can be achieved. He inspires the power and energy to get it done. — Ralph Lauren

The successful warrior is the average man with laser like focus. — Bruce Lee

A goal is not always meant to be reached; it often serves simply as something to aim at. — Bruce Lee

You are never too old to set another goal or to dream a new dream. — C. S. Lewis

Whatever you are, be a good one. — President Abraham Lincoln

If you're not sure where you are going, you're liable to end up someplace else. — Robert F. Mager

If something is important enough, even if the odds are against you, you should still do it. — Elon Musk

Whatever we plant in our subconscious mind and nourish with repetition and emotion will one day become a reality. — Earl Nightingale

When you are inspired by some great purpose, some extraordinary project, all your thoughts break their bonds. — Patanjali

Empty pockets never held anyone back. Only empty heads and empty hearts can do that. — Norman Vincent Peale

Give me a stock clerk with a goal, and I will give you a man who will make history. Give me a man without a goal and I will give you a stock clerk. — James Cash Penny

Throughout the centuries there were men who took the first steps, down new roads, armed with nothing but their own vision. — Ayn Rand

Go for the moon. If you don't get it, you'll still be heading for a star. Happiness lies to in the mere possession of money; it lies in the joy of achievement, in the thrill of the creative effort. — President Franklin D. Roosevelt

Keep your eyes on the stars and your feet on the ground. — President Theodore Roosevelt

In leadership writ large, mutually agreed upon purposes help people achieve consensus, assume responsibility, work for the common good, and build community. — Joseph Rost

In the future, there will be no female leaders. There will just be leaders. — Sheryl Sandberg

If a man knows not to which port he sails, no wind is favorable. — Seneca

Unless you give motivated people something to believe in, something bigger than their job to work toward, they will motivate themselves to find a new job and you'll be stuck with whoever's left. — Simon Sinek

If you hire people just because they can do a job, they'll work for your money. But if you hire people who believe what you believe, they'll work for you with blood and sweat and tears. — Simon Sinek

Go confidently in the direction of your dreams. Live the live you've imagined. — Henry David Thoreau

It is not what you look at that matters, it's what you see. — Henry David Thoreau

The bravest are surely those who have the clearest vision of what is before them, glory and danger alike, and yet notwithstanding, go out and meet it. — Thucydides

No dream is too big. No challenge is too great. Nothing we want for our future is beyond our reach. — President Donald J. Trump

Every great dream begins with a dreamer. Always remember, you have within you the strength, the patience and the passion to reach for the stars and to change the world. — Harriet Tubman

The two most important days in your life are the day you are born and the day you find out why. — Mark Twain

In the midst of chaos, there's is also opportunity. — Sun Tzu

Good business leaders create a vision, articulate the vision, passionately own the vision, and relentlessly drive it to completion. — Jack Welch

Yes, I am a dreamer. For a dreamer is one who can find his way by moonlight and see the dawn before the rest of the world. — Oscar Wilde

No matter what people tell you, words and ideas can change the world. — Robin Williams

You are not here merely to make a living. You are here in order to enable the world to live more amply, with greater vision, with a finer spirit of hope and achievement. You are here to enrich the world, and you impoverish yourself if you forget the errand. — President Woodrow Wilson

Too low they build, who build beneath the stars. — Edward Young

Chapter 4: Quotes About Expectations

Great leaders have high standards and set great expectations. When I was a student at Kelley School of Business at Indiana University I read an article about the link between a leader's expectations and team performance by Stanley Livingston. It was an older article then so it's ancient by today's standards. None the less, this piece had a foundational impact on my approach to leadership. Type this link into your browser to read it.
(https://hbr.org/2003/01/pygmalion-in-management)
It's still on the Harvard Business Review's site.

The quotes in this section are about expectations – What they are, how leaders set them, and how they can impact performance.

We don't rise to the level of our goals; we fall to the level of our systems. — James Clear

We aim above the mark to hit the mark. — Ralph Waldo Emerson

Be a yardstick of quality. Some people aren't used to an environment where excellence is expected. — Steve Jobs

Once you say you're going to settle for second, that's what happens to you in life. — President John F. Kennedy

The quality of a leader is reflected in the standards they set for themselves. — Ray Kroc

There is no passion to be found in settling for a life that is less than the one you are capable of living. — Nelson Mandela

The biggest temptation is to settle for too little. — Thomas Merton

The greatest danger for most of us is not that our aim is too high, and we miss it, but that it's too low and we reach it. — Michelangelo

When you raise your standards, your shoulds become your musts. — Tony Robbins

We all get what we tolerate. — Tony Robbins

Trade your expectation for appreciation and the world changes instantly. — Tony Robbins

The reasonable man adapts itself to the world; the unreasonable one persists in trying to adapt the world to himself. Therefore, all progress depends on the unreasonable man. — George Bernard Shaw

Remember that it is the actions, and not the commission, that make the officer, and that there is more expected from him, than the title. — President George Washington

Average leaders raise the bar on themselves; good leaders raise the bar for others; great leaders inspire others to raise their own bar. — Orrin Woodward

Chapter 5: Quotes about Success

This is one of my favorite sections of quotes. It's about success. This section includes quotes that leaders can use to clarify what success is and how to achieve it.

> In your actions, don't procrastinate. In your conversations, don't confuse. In your thoughts, don't wander. In your soul, don't be passive or aggressive. In your life, don't be all about business. — Marcus Aurelius

> The achievement of one goal should be the starting point of another. — Alexander Graham Bell

> Failing organizations are usually over-managed and under-led. — Warren Bennis

> Success in management requires learning as fast as the world is changing. — Warren Bennis

> The key to successful leadership is influence, not authority. — Ken Blanchard

> Destiny is not a matter of chance; it is a matter of choice. It is not a thing to be wanted for, it is a thing to be achieved. — William Jennings Bryant

Flaming enthusiasm, backed by horse sense and persistence, is the quality that most frequently makes for success — Dale Carnegie

Our greatest fear should not be of failure, but of succeeding at things in life that don't really matter. — Francis Chan

Build something 100 people love, not something one million people kind of like. — Brian Chesky

Success is walking from failure to failure with no loss of enthusiasm. — Winston Churchill

The difference between successful people and others is how long they spend feeling sorry for themselves. — Barbara Corcoran

It is not the strongest of the species that survive, nor the most intelligent, but the one most responsive to change. — Charles Darwin

The effective executive does not make staffing decisions to minimize weaknesses but to maximize strength. — Peter F. Drucker

A man is a success if he gets up in the morning and gets to bed at night, and in between he does what he wants to do. — Bob Dylan

Do not spoil what you have by desiring what you have not; remember that what you. Now have was among the things. You only hoped for. — Epicurus

There is joy in work. There is no happiness except in the realization that we have accomplished something. — Henry Ford

Wealth, like happiness, is never attained when sought after directly. It comes as a by-product of providing a useful service. —Henry Ford

If everyone is moving forward together, then success takes care of itself. — Henry Ford

Before everything else, getting ready is the secret of success. — Henry Ford

If there is any one secret of success, it lies in the ability to get the other person's point of view and see things from that person's angle as well as from your own. — Henry Ford

What man actually needs is not a tensionless state but rather the striving and struggling for a worthwhile goal, a freely chosen task. — Viktor E. Frankel

The best way to find yourself is to lose yourself in the service of others. — Mahatma Gandhi

The future depends on what you do today. Mahatma Gandhi

Patience is a key element of success. — Bill Gates

Success is a lousy teacher. It seduces smart people into thinking they can't lose. — Bill Gates

The common denominator of success is in forming the habit of doing things that failures don't like to do. — Albert Gray

Everyone enjoys doing the kind of work for which he is best suited. — Napoleon Hill

Don't ever promise more than you can deliver, but always deliver more than you promise. — Lou Holtz

Winners and losers aren't born, they are the products of how they think. — Lou Holtz

The man who complains about the way the ball bounces is likely the one who dropped it — Lou Holtz

If you only care enough for a result, you almost certainly attain it. If you wish to be rich you will be rich, if you wish to be learned you will be learned. If you wish to be good you will be good. Only you must then really wish these things and wish them exclusively and not wish at the same time hundred other incompatible things just as strongly. — William James

All success begins with self-discipline. It starts with you. — Dwayne Johnson

Optimism is the faith that leads to achievement. — Helen Keller

Victory has a hundred fathers and defeat is an orphan. –- President John F. Kennedy

There will come a time when you believe everything is finished. That will be the beginning. — Louis L'Amour

I've never dreamt of success. I worked for it. — Estee Lauder

Life is what happens while you're busy making other plans. — John Lennon

Don't worry when you are not recognized but strive to be worthy of recognition. — President Abraham Lincoln

A good criterion for measuring success in life is the number of people you have made happy. — Robert J. Lumsden

Whoever desires constant success must change his conduct with the times. — Niccolò Machiavelli

Successful and unsuccessful people do not vary greatly in their abilities. They vary in their desire to reach their potential. — John C. Maxwell

The tragedy in life doesn't lie in not reaching your goal. The tragedy lies in having no goal to reach. — Benjamin Mays

To succeed in life, you need three things: a wishbone, a backbone, and a funny bone. — Reba McEntire

The only honest measure of your success is what you are doing compared with your true potential. — Paul J. Meyer

Success is the progressive realization of a worthy ideal. — Earl Nightingale

We need to internalize this idea of excellence. Not many folks spend a lot of time trying to be excellent. — President Barack H. Obama

Chance favors the prepared mind. — Louis Pasteur

Action is the foundational key to all success. — Pablo Picasso

There are no secrets to success. It is the result of preparation, hard work, and learning from failure. — General Colin Powell

We must never be afraid to go too far, for success lies just beyond. — Marcel Proust

I know of no single formula for success. But over the years I have observed that some attributes of leadership are universal and are often about finding ways of encouraging people to combine their efforts, their talents, their insights, their enthusiasm and their inspiration to work together. — Queen Elizabeth II

The ladder of success is best climbed by stepping on the rungs of opportunity. — Ayn Rand

I can give you a six-word formula for success: Think things through — then follow through. — Edward Rickenbacker

The path to success is to take massive, determined actions. — Tony Robbins

To be a champ, you have to believe in yourself when no one else will. — Sugar Ray Robinson

The secret of success is to do the common thing uncommonly well. — John D. Rockefeller

Don't wish it was easier, wish you were better. Don't wish for less problems, wish for more skills. Don't wish for less challenges, wish for more wisdom. The major value in life is not what you get. The major value in life is what you become. Success is not to be pursued; it is to be attracted by the person you become. — Jim Rohn

The most important single ingredient in the formula of success is knowing how to get along with people. — President Theodore Roosevelt

The only place where success comes before work is in the dictionary. — Vidal Sasson

Winners are the ones who really listen to the truth of their heart. — Sylvester Stallone

Definiteness of purpose is the starting point of all achievement. — W. Clement Stone

I can't give you a surefire formula for success, but I can give you a formula for failure: try to please everybody all the time. — Herbert Bayard Swope

Things change for the better when we take responsibility for our own thoughts, decisions and actions. — Eric Thomas Ph. D.

A man is rich in proportion to the number of things he can afford to let alone. — Henry David Thoreau

In the end, you're measured not by how much you undertake but by what you finally accomplish. — President Donald J. Trump

What separates the winners from the losers is how a person reacts to each new twist of fate. — President Donald J. Trump

You can be the ripest, juiciest peach in the world and there are still going to be some people who hate peaches. — Dita Von Teese

Success at the highest level comes down to one question: Can you decide that your happiness can come from someone else's success? — Bill Walton

Before you are a leader, success is all about growing yourself. When you become a leader, success is all about growing others. — Jack Welch

If you don't make mistakes, you're not working on hard enough problems. And that's a big mistake. — Frank Wilczek

The most successful people reach the top not because they are free of limitations, but because they act in spite of their limitations. — Michael K. Williams

A champion is defined not by their wins, but by how they recover when they fail. — Serena Williams

You know when you are on the road to success if you would do your job and not be paid for it. — Oprah Winfrey

Success comes from knowing that you did your best to become the best that you are capable of becoming. — John Wooden

Don't measure yourself by what you have accomplished, but by what you should have accomplished with your ability. — John Wooden

I know the price of success: dedication, hard work, and an unremitting devotion to the things you want to see happen. — Frank Lloyd Wright

The real opportunity for success lies within the person and not in the job. — Zig Ziglar

You can have everything in life you want, if you will just help other people get what they want. — Zig Ziglar

What you get by achieving your goals is not as important as what you come by achieving your goals. — Zig Ziglar

Chapter 6: Quotes about Attitude

Great leaders must be aware of their attitude and the impact has on those who lead. Often our attitude is guided by what we think we can control. Recognizing the extent of our control over events, situations and other people is the first step in managing our own attitude. This section contains dozens of excellent quotes about developing a great attitude and your attitude's impact.

He who believes is strong; he who doubts is weak. Strong convictions precede great actions. — Louisa May Alcott

We all have our own life to pursue, our own kind of dream to be weaving, and we all have the power to make wishes come true, as long as we keep believing. — Louisa May Alcott

I am the greatest. I said that even before I knew I was. — Muhammad Ali

Nothing is hopeless that is right. — Susan B. Anthony

The greatest pollution problem we face today is negativity. Eliminate the negative attitude and believe you can do anything. — Mary Kay Ash

Don't let the negatives of life control you. Rise above them. Use them as your steppingstones to go higher than you ever dreamed possible. — Mary Kay Ash

You have power over your mind — not outside events. Realize this, and you will find strength. — Marcus Aurelius

A man's life is what his thoughts make of it. — Marcus Aurelius

The more I want to get something done, the less I call it work. — Richard Bach

Enthusiasm moves the world. — Arthur Balfour

To guarantee success, act as if it were impossible to fail. — Dorthea Brande

Don't let someone else's opinion become your reality. — Les Brown

Ah, but a man's reach should exceed his grasp. Or what's a heaven for? — Robert Browning

The mind is everything. What you think you become. — Buddha

Only I can change my life. No one can do it for me. — Carol Burnett

When you reach for the stars you may not quite get one, but you won't come up with a handful of mud either. — Leo Burnett

People say that what we are seeking is a meaning for life. I don't think this is what we're really seeking. I think what we're seeking is an experience of being alive. — Joseph Campbell

We cannot cure the world of sorrows, but we can choose to live in joy. — Joseph Campbell

We must let go of the life we planned so as to accept the one that is waiting for us. — Joseph Campbell

Follow your bliss and the universe will open doors where there were only walls. — Joseph Campbell

Don't worry about failures, worry about the chances you miss when you don't even try. — Jack Canfield

The trick is in what one emphasizes. We either make ourselves miserable or we make ourselves strong. The amount of work is the same. — Carlos Castaneda

How you think when you lose determines how long it will be until you win. — G. K. Chesterton

A pessimist sees the difficulty in every opportunity; an optimist sees the opportunity in every difficulty. — Winston Churchill

The limits of the possible can only be defined by going beyond them into the impossible. — Arthur C. Clarke

And when you want something, all the universe conspires in helping you achieve it. — Paul Coelho

But until a person can say deeply and honestly, "I am what I am today because of the choices I made yesterday," that person cannot say, "I choose otherwise." — Stephen Covey

We must believe that we are gifted for something, and that this thing, at whatever cost, must be attained. — Marie Curie

If you have good thoughts, they will shine out of your face like sunbeams and you will always look lovely. — Roald Dahl

I can't change the direction of the wind, but I can adjust my sails to always reach my destination. — Jimmy Dean

I think therefore I am. — Reneé Descartes

You either run with lions or walk with sheep. — Matshona Dhliwayo

Life is too short to be small. — Benjamin Disraeli

The important thing is this: to be able to give up in any given moment all that we are for what we can become. — Charles Du Bos

People seldom do what they believe in. They do what is convenient, then repent — Bob Dylan

Never interrupt someone doing something you said couldn't be done. — Amelia Earhart

What lies behind us and what lies before us are tiny matters compared to what is within us. — Ralph Waldo Emerson

People only see what they are prepared to see. — Ralph Waldo Emerson

A man is what he thinks about all day long. — Ralph Waldo Emerson

The only person you are destined to become is the person you decide to be. — Ralph Waldo Emerson

Nothing great was ever achieved without enthusiasm. — Ralph Waldo Emerson

It's not what happens to you, but how you react to it that matters. — Epictetus

Circumstances don't make the man; they only reveal him to himself. — Epictetus

Don't seek for everything to happen as you wish it would, but rather wish that everything happens as it actually will – then your life will flow well. — Epictetus

There is no man living that cannot do more than he thinks he can. — Henry Ford

I cannot discover that anyone knows enough to say definitely what is and what is not possible. — Henry Ford

Whether you believe you can do a thing or not, you are right. — Henry Ford

You must not under any pretense allow your mind to dwell on any thought that is not positive, constructive, optimistic, kind. — Emmet Fox

Be fit for more than the thing you are now doing. Let everyone know that you have a reserve in yourself, — that you have more power than you are now using. If you are not too large for the place you occupy, you are too small for it. — President James A. Garfield

Always be a first-rate version of yourself instead of a second-rate version of somebody else. — Judy Garland

Be faithful to that which exists within yourself. — Andre Gide

There is a vitality, a life force, an energy that is translated through you; and because there is only one of you in all of time, this expression is unique. — Martha Graham

Build your own dreams, or someone else will hire you to build theirs. — Farrah Gray

Don't be afraid your life will end; be afraid it will never begin. — Grace Hansen

Focused mind power is one of the strongest forces on earth. — Mark Victor Hansen

What lies behind us and what lies before us are tiny matters compared to what lies within us. — Henry Haskins

I am the master of my fate; I am the captain of my soul. — William Ernest Henley

Nothing is impossible. The word itself says 'I'm possible!' — Audrey Hepburn

Whatever the mind of man can conceive and believe, it can achieve. — Napoleon Hill

Like the wind that carries one ship east and another west, the law of autosuggestion will lift you up or pull you down according to the way that you set your sails of thought. — Napoleon Hill

There is another apt Latin expression: Materiam superabat opus. (The workmanship is better than the material.) The material we've been given genetically, emotionally, financially, that's where we begin. We don't control that. We do control what we make of that material, and whether we squander it. — Ryan Holiday

Ability is what you're capable of doing. Motivation determines what you do. Attitude determines how well you do it. — Lou Holtz

I can't believe that God put us on this earth to be ordinary. — Lou Holtz

Nothing is as good as it seems, and nothing is as bad as it seems. Somewhere in between lies realty. — Lou Holtz

Being an optimist after you've got the very thing you want doesn't count. — Kin Hubbard

Little minds are tamed and subdued by misfortune, but great minds rise above them. — Washington Irving

Act if what you do makes a difference. It does. — William James

It is our attitude at the beginning of a difficult task which, more than anything else, will affect its successful outcome. — William James

The greatest discovery of my generation is that human beings can alter their lives by altering their attitudes of mind. — William James

Nothing can stop the man with the right mental attitude from achieving his goal; nothing on earth can help the man with the wrong mental attitude. — President Thomas Jefferson

Nothing gives a person so much advantage over another as to remain always cool and unruffled under all circumstances. — President Thomas Jefferson

Be humble. Be hungry. And be the hardest worker in the room. — Dwayne Johnson

Some people want it to happen, some wish it would happen, others make it happen. — Michael Jordan

Sometimes you just have to put on lip gloss and pretend to be psyched. — Mindy Kaling

Security is mostly a superstition. Life is either a daring adventure, or nothing. — Helen Keller

Keep your face to the sunshine and you cannot see a shadow. — Helen Keller

We are not makers of history; we are made by history. — Dr. Martin Luther King Jr.

Get busy living or get busy dying. — Stephen King

Man is so made that when anything fires his soul, impossibilities vanish. — Jean de La Fontaine

The consciousness of self is the greatest hindrance to the proper execution of all physical action. — Bruce Lee

Always bear in mind that your own resolution to succeed is more important than any one thing. — President Abraham Lincoln

There is no security on the Earth, there is only opportunity. — General Douglas MacArthur

I'm not interested in preserving the status quo; I want to overthrow it. — Niccolò Machiavelli

Where the willingness is great, the difficulties cannot be great. — Niccolò Machiavelli

Excellence is not a skill it's an attitude. — Ralph Marston

Lord, grant that I may always desire more than I can accomplish. — Michelangelo

One person with a belief is equal to 99 who have only interests. — John Steward Mill

Our attitude towards life determines life's attitude toward us. — Earl Nightingale

If you aren't going all the way, why go at all? — Joe Namath

Once you replace negative thoughts with positive ones, you'll start having positive results. — Willie Nelson

Our attitude towards life determines life's attitude toward us. — Earl Nightingale

We become what we think about. — Earl Nightingale

A lot of times, people look at the negative side of what they feel they can't do. I always look on the positive side of what I can do. — Chuck Norris

Work like you don't need the money. Love like you've never been hurt. Dance like nobody's watching. — Satchel Paige

Change your thoughts and change your world. — Norman Vincent Peale

This is one of the greatest laws in the universe. Fervently do I wish I had discovered it as a very young man. It dawned upon me much later in life and I've found it to be one of the greatest, if not my greatest discovery outside of my relationship with God. And the great law briefly and simply stated is that if you think in negative terms, you'll get negative results. If you think in positive terms, you will achieve positive results. That is the simple fact which is at the basis of an astonishing law of prosperity and success in three words "believe and succeed." — Norman Vincent Peale

If your past is limited, your future is boundless. — President Franklin Pierce

Reality is created in the mind; we can change our reality by changing our mind. — Plato

What we achieve inwardly will change outer reality. — Plutarch

Limit your always and your never. — Amy Poehler

Your present circumstances don't determine where you can go; they merely determine where you start. — Nido Qubein

There are no constraints on the human mind, no walls around the human spirit, no barriers to our progress except those we ourselves erect. — President Ronald Reagan

If you have a positive attitude and constantly strive to give your best effort, eventually you will overcome your immediate problems and find you are ready for greater challenges. — Pat Riley

Believe you can and you're halfway there. — President Theodore Roosevelt

Inspiration comes from within yourself. One has to be positive. When you're positive, good things happen. — Deep Roy

Never underestimate the power of dreams and the influence of the human spirit. We are all the same in this notion: The potential for greatness lives within each of us. — Wilma Rudolph

Every strike brings me closer to the next home run. — Babe Ruth

I learned that if you want to make it bad enough, no matter how bad it is, you can make it. — Gayle Sayers

A man can succeed at almost anything for which he has unlimited enthusiasm. — Charles M. Schwab

It is not in the stars to hold our destiny, but in ourselves. — William Shakespeare

Life is 10% what happens to you and 90% how you react to it. — Charles Swindoll

When you want to succeed as bad as you want. To breathe, then you'll be successful. — Eric Thomas Ph. D.

Winners make a habit of manufacturing their own positive expectations in advance of the event. — Brian Tracy

I am an old man and have known a great many troubles, but most of them never happened. — Mark Twain

If you realize that all things change, there is nothing you will try to hold on to. If you are not afraid of dying, there is nothing you cannot achieve. — Lao Tzu

They can conquer who believe they can. — Virgil

We are what we pretend to be, so we must be careful about what we pretend to be. — Kurt Vonnegut

The winners in life think constantly in terms of I can, I will, I am. Losers, on the other hand, concentrated their waking thoughts on what they should have or would have done, or what they can't do. — Dennis Waitley

The most common way people give up their power is by thinking they don't have any. — Alice Walker

99% of failures come from people who make excuses. — President George Washington

Happiness depends more upon the internal frame of a person's own mind, than on the externals in the world. — President George Washington

The greater part of our misery or unhappiness is determined not by our circumstance, but by our disposition. — Martha Washington
Keep your face always toward the sunshine and shadows will fall behind you. — Walt Whitman

Our deepest fear is that we are powerful beyond measure. — Marianne Williamson

There is no such thing as failure. Failure is just life trying to move us in another direction. — Oprah Winfrey

With the right kind of coaching and determination you can accomplish anything. — Reese Witherspoon

Do not let what you cannot do interfere with what you can do. — John Wooden

Things work out best for those who make the best of how things work out. — John Wooden

If you can dream it, you can achieve it. — Zig Ziglar

You were born to win, but to be a winner, you must plan to win, prepare to win, and expect to win. — Zig Ziglar

People often say that motivation doesn't last. Well, neither does bathing - that's why we recommend it daily. — Zig Ziglar

Chapter 7: Quotes About Execution and Impact

Execution is a yardstick by how leaders are measured. How well did the team execute the plan? This chapter describes execution, habits and getting things done.

Do the things you know, and you shall learn the truth you need to know. — Louisa May Alcott

I am not afraid of an army of lions led by a sheep. I am afraid of an army of sheep led by a lion. — Alexander the Great

If everything seems under control, you're not going fast enough. — Mario Andretti

We don't rise to the level of our expectations; we fall to the level of our training. — Archilochus

Quality is not an act; it is a habit. — Aristotle

We are what we repeatedly do. Excellence, then, is not an act, but a habit. — Aristotle

What it lies in our power to do, it lies in our power not to do. — Aristotle

It's attention to detail that make the difference between average and stunning. — Francis Atterbury

What we do now echoes in eternity — Marcus Aurelius

Everything we hear is an opinion, not a fact. Everything we see is a perspective, not the truth. — Marcus Aurelius

Concentrate all your thoughts upon the work in hand. The sun's rays do not burn until brought to a focus. — Alexander Graham Bell

Think like a man of action, act like a man of thought. — Henri Bergson

An expert is a person who has made all the mistakes that can be made in a very narrow field. — Niels Bohr

Never interrupt your enemy when he is making a mistake. — Napoléon Bonaparte

Execution is the ability to mesh strategy with reality, align people with goals, and achieve the promised results. — Lawrence Bossidy

The secret of enjoying work is contained in one word - excellence. To know how to do something well is to enjoy it. — Pearl Buck

Greatness is more than potential. It is the execution of that potential. Beyond the raw talent. You need the appropriate training. You need the discipline. You need the inspiration. You need the drive. — Eric A. Burns

Clarity and simplicity are the antidotes to complexity and uncertainty. — General George Casey

Do not reveal what you have thought upon doing, but by wise council keep it secret being determined to carry it into execution. — Chanakya

Do your own thinking independently. Be the chess player, not the chess piece. — Ralph Charell

Know the true value of time; snatch, seize and enjoy every minute of it. — Lord Chesterfield

There's no difference between a pessimist who says, "Oh, it's hopeless, so don't bother doing anything," and an optimist who says, "Don't bother doing anything, it's going to turn out fine anyway." Either way, nothing happens. — Yvon Chouinard

The price of greatness is responsibility. — Winston Churchill

Some people dream of success while others wake up and work hard at it. — Winston Churchill

Good is the enemy of great. — Jim Collins

Those who trust to chance must abide by the results of chance. — President Calvin Coolidge

What you do has far greater impact that what you say. — Stephen Covey

Always look for the fool in the deal. If you don't find one, it's you. — Mark Cuban

Someday is not a day of the week. — Janet Dailey

Small opportunities are often the beginning of great enterprises. — Demosthenes

Citius, Altius, Fortius. — Henri Martin Didon, The Olympic Motto

I have been impressed with the urgency of doing. Knowing is not enough; we must apply. Being willing is not enough; we must do. — Leonardo Da Vinci

It had long since come to my attention that people of accomplishment rarely sat back and let things happen to them. They went out and happened to things. — Leonardo Da Vinci

A schedule defends from chaos and whim. — Annie Dillard

The way to get started and to begin is doing. — Walt Disney

If you can dream it, you can do it. And always remember that this whole thing was started by a mouse. — Walt Disney

First, think. Second, dream. Third, believe. And finally, dare. — Walt Disney

If you focus on results, you'll never change. If you focus on change, you'll get results. — Jack Dixon

Time is the scarcest resource, and unless it is managed, nothing else can be managed. — Peter F. Drucker

What gets measured gets managed. — Peter F. Drucker

If you can't measure it, you can't improve it. — Peter F. Drucker

I have never encountered an executive who remains effective while tackling more than two tasks at a time. — Peter F. Drucker

Problem solving, however necessary, does not produce results. It prevents damage. Exploiting opportunities produces results. — Peter F. Drucker

If we did all the things we are capable of, we would literally astound ourselves. — Thomas A. Edison

I have never encountered an executive who remains effective while tackling more than two tasks at a time. — Peter F. Drucker

Problem solving, however necessary, does not produce results. It prevents damage. Exploiting opportunities produces results. — Peter F. Drucker

No excuses. No explanation. You don't win on emotion. You win on execution. — Tony Dungy

The most effective way to do it is to do it. — Amelia Earhart

Fast is fine, but accuracy is everything. — Wyatt Earp

If we did all the things we are capable of, we would literally astound ourselves. — Thomas A. Edison

Everything should be made as simple as possible, but not simpler. — Albert Einstein

Strive not to be a success, but rather to be of value. — Albert Einstein

You have to learn the rules of the game. And then, you have to play it better than anyone else. — Albert Einstein

Motivation is the art of getting people to do what you want them to do because they want to do it. — President Dwight D. Eisenhower

First say to yourself what you would be; and then do what you have to do. — Epictetus

Conditions are never perfect. 'Someday' is a disease that will take your dreams to the grave with you...If it's important to you and you want to do it 'eventually' just do it and correct course along the way. — Tim Ferriss

The first principle is that you must not fool yourself, and you are the easiest person to fool. — Richard P Feynman

It has been my observation that most people get ahead during the time that others waste. — Henry Ford

How wonderful it is that nobody need wait a single moment before starting to improve the world. — Anne Frank

To succeed, jump as quickly at opportunities as you do at conclusions. – Benjamin Franklin

The first rule of any technology used in a business is that automation applied to an efficient operation will magnify the efficiency. The second is that automation applied to an inefficient operation will magnify the inefficiency. — Bill Gates

Innovation is rewarded. Execution is worshipped. — Dan Gilbert

Your grammar is a reflection of your image. Good or bad, you have made an impression. And like all impressions, you are in total control. — Jeffrey Gitomer

Competent people are the most resistant to change. — Seth Godin

There's no shortage of remarkable ideas; what's missing is the will to execute them. — Seth Godin

Ideas are yesterday, execution is today, and excellence will see you into tomorrow. — Julian Hall

Haste in every business brings failures. — Herodotus

Don't wait. The time will never be just right. — Napoleon Hill

When all is said and done, more is said than done. — Lou Holtz

You're never as good as everyone tells you when you win, and you're never as bad as they say when you lose. — Lou Holtz

Words without actions are the assassins of idealism. — President Herbert Hoover

Don't think, just do. — Horace

Any man worth his salt will stick up for what he believes right, but it takes a slightly better man to acknowledge instantly and without reservation that he is in error. — President Andrew Jackson

Do you want to know who you are? Don't ask. Act! Action will delineate and define you. — President Thomas Jefferson

Determine never to be idle. No person will have occasion to complain of the want of time who never loses any. It is wonderful how much may be done if we are always doing. — President Thomas Jefferson

To me, ideas are worth nothing unless executed. They are just a multiplier. Execution is worth millions. — Steve Jobs

The last 10% it takes to launch something takes as much energy as the first 90%. — Rob Kalin

The time to repair the roof is when the sun is shining. — President John F. Kennedy

Happiness is not something ready-made. It comes from your own actions. — Dalai Lama

A year from now you will wish you had started today. — Karen Lamb

One does not accumulate but eliminate. It is not daily increase but daily decrease. The height of cultivation always runs to simplicity. — Bruce Lee

Be with a leader when he is right, stay with him when he is still right, but, leave him when he is wrong. — President Abraham Lincoln

We generate fears while we sit. We overcome them by action. Fear is nature's way of warning us to get busy. — Dr. Henry Link

Perfection is not attainable, but if we chase perfection we can catch excellence. — Vince Lombardi

Never give an order that can't be obeyed. — General Douglas MacArthur

The first method for estimating the intelligence of a ruler is to look at the men around him. — Niccolò Machiavelli

The higher you want to climb, the more you need leadership. The greater the impact you want to make, the greater your influence needs to be. — John C. Maxwell

Never doubt that a small group of thoughtful committed citizens can change the world. Indeed, it is the only thing that ever has. — Margaret Mead

I alone cannot change the world, but I can cast a stone across the water to create many ripples. — Mother Teresa

The man of thought who will not act is ineffective; the man of action who will not think is dangerous. — President Richard M. Nixon

Change will not come if we wait for some other person or some other time. We are the one's we've been waiting for. We are the change we seek. — President Barack H. Obama

It is vain to do with more what can be done with less. — William of Occam

Time is what we want most, but what we use worst. — William Penn

A competent leader can get efficient service from poor troops, while on the contrary, an incapable leader can demoralize the best of troops. — General John J. Pershing

There are two kinds of failures: those who thought and never did, and those who did and never thought. — Laurence J. Peter

The thing that keeps a business ahead of the competition is excellence in execution. — Tom Peters

Only put off until tomorrow what you are willing to die having left undone. — Pablo Picasso

Remember that time is money. — President Franklin Pierce

The beginning is the most important part of the work. — Plato

Knowledge, if it does not determine action, is dead to us. — Plotinus

The essence of strategy is choosing what not to do. — Michael Porter

Strategy equals execution. — General Colin Powell

Don't be afraid to give up the good and go for the great. — Steve Prefontaine

When deeds speak, words are nothing. — Pierre-Joseph Proudhon

If you spend your life trying to be good at everything, you will never be great at anything. — Tom Rath

Complexity is the enemy of execution. — Tony Robbins

Life is not a spectator sport. — Jackie Robinson

It takes as much energy to wish as it does to plan. — Elanor Roosevelt

It is not the critic who counts; not the man who points out how the strong man stumbles, or where the doer of deeds could have done them better. The credit belongs to the man who is actually in the arena, whose face is marred by dust and sweat and blood; who strives valiantly; who errs, who comes short again and again, because there is no effort without error and shortcoming; but who does actually strive to do the deeds; who knows great enthusiasms, the great devotions; who spends himself in a worthy cause; who at the best knows in the end the triumph of high achievement, and who at the worst, if he fails, at least fails while daring greatly, so that his place shall never be with those cold and timid souls who neither know victory nor defeat. — President Theodore Roosevelt

Yesterday's home runs don't win today's games. — Babe Ruth

The mark of a great man is one who knows when to set aside the important things in order to accomplish the vital ones. — Brandon Sanderson

Readied and waiting.   The readiness is all. — William Shakespeare

Ideation without execution is delusion. — Robin S. Sharma

Don't wait until you are ready to take action, take action to be ready. — Jensen Siaw

Don't write so that you can be understood, write so that you can't be misunderstood. — President William Howard Taft

Don't follow the crowd, let the crowd follow you. — Margaret Thatcher

You must not only aim right but draw the bow with all your might. — Henry David Thoreau

Remember, there's no such thing as an unrealistic goal—just unrealistic time frames. President Donald J. Trump

As long as you're going to be thinking anyway, think big. — President Donald J. Trump

Don't raise your voice. Improve your argument. — Desmond Tutu

The secret of getting ahead is getting started. — Mark Twain

Everyone has a plan until they get punched in the mouth. — Mike Tyson

Opportunities multiply as they are seized. — Sun Tzu

When it all comes down to it, nothing trumps execution. — Gary Vaynerchuck

Knowing is not enough; we must apply. Wishing is not enough; we must do. — Johann Wolfgang von Goethe

What is not started will never get finished. — Johann Wolfgang von Goethe

There is only one boss. The customer. And he can fire everybody in the company, from the chairman on down, simply by spending his money somewhere else. — Sam Walton

As of this second, quit doing less than excellent work. — Thomas J. Watson

Those who let things happen usually lose to those who make things happen. — Dave Weinbaum

Change before you have to. — Jack Welch

There are two ways of spreading light: to be the candle or the mirror that reflects it. — Edith Wharton

We convince by our presence. — Walt Whitman

There is nothing more uncommon than common sense. — Frank Lloyd Wright

Life does not consist in thinking; it consists in acting. — President Woodrow Wilson

Make each day your masterpiece — John Wooden

If you don't have time to do it right, when will you have time to do it over? — John Wooden

Failure is not fatal, but failure to change might be. — John Wooden

Chapter 8: Quotes About Grit and Perseverance

Leaders need to be gritty and must be able to encourage their teammates to persevere. This section contains quotes about overcoming obstacles to succeed.

Nothing will work unless you do. — Maya Angelou

There is nothing impossible to him who will try. — Alexander the Great

Our greatest glory is not in never failing, but in rising every time we fail. — Antiochus

For every failure there's an alternative course of action. you just have to find it. — Mary Kay Ash

Start by doing what's necessary; then do what's possible; and suddenly you're doing the impossible. — St. Francis of Assisi

When one door closes another one opens; but we so often look so long and so regretfully upon the closed door, that we do not see the ones which open for us — Alexander Graham Bell

I knew that if I failed, I wouldn't regret that, but I knew the one thing I might regret is not trying. — Jeff Bezos

The reason most people fail instead of succeed is they trade what they want most for what they want at the moment. — Napoléon Bonaparte

Ambition is the path to success. Persistence is the vehicle you arrive in. — Senator Bill Bradley

The Wright brothers flew through the smoke screen of impossibility. — Dorthea Brande

The best preparation for tomorrow is doing your best today. — H. Jackson Brown, Jr.

You are never too old to set another goal or to dream a new dream. — Les Brown

I believe that life is a journey, often difficult and sometimes incredibly cruel, but we are well equipped for it if only we tap into our talents and gifts and allow them to blossom. — Les Brown

If opportunity doesn't knock, build a door. — Milton Burle

When you have a dream, you've got to grab it and never let go. — Carol Burnett

Permanence, perseverance and persistence in spite of all obstacles, discouragements and impossibilities. It is this, that in all things distinguishes the strong souls from the weak. — Thomas Carlisle

Every noble work is at first impossible. — Thomas Carlisle

If you're going through hell, keep going. — Winston Churchill

Mountaintops inspire leaders but valleys mature them. — Winston Churchill

Honor lies in honest toil. — President Grover Cleveland

If you live long enough, you'll make mistakes. But if you learn from them, you'll be a better person. It's how you handle adversity, not how it affects you. The main thing is never quit, never quit, never quit. — President William J. Clinton

The only failure is not to try. — George Clooney

A professional is a person who can do his best at a time when he doesn't particularly feel like it. — Alistair Cooke

Nothing in the world can take the place of Persistence. Talent will not; nothing is more common than unsuccessful men with talent. Genius will not; unrewarded genius is almost a proverb. Education will not; the world is full of educated derelicts. Persistence and Determination alone are omnipotent. The slogan "Press On" has solved and will always solve the problems of the human race. — President Calvin Coolidge

Obstacles are things a person sees when he takes his eyes off his goal. — E. Joseph Cossman

More men have become great by practice than by nature. — Democritus

I hate that word: lucky. It cheapens a lot of hard work. — Peter Dinklage

Action may not always bring happiness, but there is not happiness without action. — Benjamin Disraeli

The most difficult thing is the decision to act, the rest is merely tenacity. — Amelia Earhart

I have not failed. I've just found 10,000 ways that won't work. — Thomas A. Edison

Reality is merely an illusion, albeit a very persistent one. — Albert Einstein

A problem is a chance for your to do your best. — Duke Ellington

Both my mother and I were determined that we weren't going to stay on welfare. We always worked toward...having a better life. We never had any doubts that we would. — Larry Ellison

Just don't give up trying to do what you really want to do. Where there is love and inspiration, I don't think you can go wrong. — Ella Fitzgerald

If you have no critics, you'll likely have no success. — Malcolm Forbes

Whenever everything seems to be going against you, remember that the airplane takes off against the wind, not with it. — Henry Ford

Failure is simply the opportunity to begin again, this time more intelligently. — Henry Ford

There are no big problems, there are just a lot of little problems. — Henry Ford

Energy and persistence conquer all things. — Benjamin Franklin

Diligence is the mother of good luck. — Benjamin Franklin

The best way out is always through. — Robert Frost

It's fine to celebrate success, but it is more important to heed the lessons of failure. — Bill Gates

There are no working hours for leaders. — James Cardinal Gibbons

There's no lotion or potion that will make sales faster and easier for you - unless your potion is hard work. — Jeffrey Gitomer

Hard work doesn't guarantee success, but it improves its chances. — B. J. Gupta

When I hear somebody sigh, 'Life is hard,' I am always tempted to ask, 'Compared to what?' — Sydney J. Harris

The road to success is not easy to navigate, but with hard work, drive and passion, it's possible to achieve the American dream. — Tommy Hilfiger

Winners embrace hard work. They love the discipline of it, the tradeoff they're making to win. Losers, on the other hand, see it as punishment. And that's the difference. — Lou Holtz

It's not the load that breaks you down, it's the way you carry it. — Lou Holtz

I find the harder I work the more luck I seem to have. — President Thomas Jefferson

Great works are performed not by strength but by perseverance. — Samuel Johnson

I've failed over and over again in my life. And that is why I succeed. — Michael Jordan

I can accept failure; everyone fails at something. But I can't accept not trying. — Michael Jordan

It doesn't matter if you try and try and try again and fail. It does matter if you try and fail and fail to try again. — Charles Kettering

Even if you fall on your face, you're still moving forward. — Victor Kiam

If you can't fly, then run; if you can't run, then walk; if you can't walk, then crawl; but whatever you do, you have to keep moving forward. — Dr. Martin Luther King Jr.

Luck is a dividend of sweat. The more you sweat, the luckier you get. — Ray Kroc

Remember that not getting what you want is sometimes a wonderful stroke of luck. — Dalai Lama

Opportunities are usually disguised as hard work, so most people don't recognize them. — Ann Landers

Some of the world's greatest feats were accomplished by people not smart enough to know they were impossible. — Doug Larson

Hardships often prepare ordinary people for an extraordinary destiny. — C. S. Lewis

You can't go back and change the beginning, but you can start where you are and change the ending. — C. S. Lewis

I walk slowly, but never backward. — President Abraham Lincoln

No matter what you're going through, there's a light at the end of the tunnel. — Demi Lovato

Constant dripping hollows out a stone. — Lucretius

It always seems impossible until it's done. — Nelson Mandela

A winner is a dreamer who never gives up. — Nelson Mandela

Happiness is not the absence of problems; it's the ability to deal with them. — Steve Maraboli

Half-heartedness never won a battle. — President William McKinley

It's not about perfect. It's about effort. And when you bring that effort every single day, that's where transformation happens. — Jillian Michaels

Hardship is the native soil of manhood and self-reliance. — John Neal

That which does not kill us makes us stronger. — Fredrich Nietzsche

I attribute my success to this: I never gave or took any excuse. — Florence Nightingale

Defeat doesn't finish a man, quit does. A man is not finished when he's defeated. He's finished when he quits. — President Richard M. Nixon

The finest steel has to go through the hottest fire. — President Richard M. Nixon

You can't let your failures define you. You have to let your failures teach you. — President Barack H. Obama

Progress will come in fits and starts. It's not always a straight line. It's not always smooth path. — President Barack H. Obama

If you're walking down the right path and you're willing to keep walking, eventually you'll make progress. — President Barack H. Obama

If you work really hard and you're kind, amazing things will happen. — Conan O'Brien

Work hard in silence, let success be your noise. — Frank Ocean

We all have dreams. But in order to make dreams come into reality, it takes an awful lot of determination, dedication, self-discipline and effort. — Jesse Owens

Always make a total effort, even when the odds are against you. — Arnold Palmer

Let me tell you the secret that has led me to my goals: my strength lies solely in my tenacity. — Louis Pasteur

If you are going to win any battle, you have to do one thing: You have to make the mind run the body. Never let the body tell the mind what to do. The body is never tired if the mind is not tired. — General George S. Patton Jr.

Most people give up just when they are about to achieve success. They quit on the one-yard line. They give up at the last minute of the game, one foot from a winning touchdown. — H. Ross Perot

To give anything less than your best is to sacrifice the gift. — Steve Prefontaine

I think the thing about that was I was always willing to work; I was not the fastest player or the biggest player but I was determined to be the best football player I could be on the football field and I think I was able to accomplish that through hard work. — Jerry Rice

Do all that you can with all you have, wherever you are. — President Theodore Roosevelt

It's hard to beat a person who never gives up. — Babe Ruth

Every truth passes through three stages before it is recognized. In the first, it is ridiculed. In the second, it is opposed. In the third, it is regarded as self-evident. — Arthur Schopenhauer

It is a rough road that leads to the heights of greatness. — Seneca

The pressure of adversity does not affect the mind of the brave man. It is more powerful than external circumstances. — Seneca

People are always blaming their circumstances for what they are. I don't believe in circumstances. The people who get on in this world are the people who get up and look for the circumstances they want and if they can't find them make them. — George Bernard Shaw

Nothing great was ever done without much enduring. — St Catherine of Siena

There are no traffic jams along the extra mile. — Roger Staubach

Timing, perseverance, and 10 years of trying will eventually make you look like an overnight success. — Biz Stone

I do not know anyone who has gotten to the top without hard work. That is the recipe. It will not always get you to the top but should get you pretty near. — Margaret Thatcher

America was not built on fear. America was built on courage, on imagination, and an unbeatable determination to do the job at hand. — President Harry S. Truman

We live in the kind of society where, in almost all cases, hard work is rewarded. — Neil deGrasse Tyson

Being defeated is often a temporary condition. Giving up is what makes it permanent. — Marilyn Vos Savant

Just keep going. Everybody gets better if they keep at it. — Ted Williams

The man who is swimming against the stream knows the strength of it. — President Woodrow Wilson

Chapter 9 Quotes About Gratitude

The quotes in this section highlight the role and impact that gratitude can have for a great leader.

I've learned that you shouldn't go through life with a catcher's mitt on both hands; you need to be able to throw something back. — Maya Angelou

From what we get, we can make a living, what we give, however, makes a life. — Arthur Ashe

Do not indulge in dreams of having what you have not, but recon up the chief of the blessings you do possess, and then thankfully remember how you would crave for them if they were not yours. — Marcus Aurelius

When it comes to life, the critical thing is whether you take things for granted or take them with gratitude. — G. K. Chesterton

We make a living by what we get, but we make a life by what we give. — Winston Churchill

Some people are always grumbling because roses have thorns; I am thankful that thorns have roses. — Alphose Karr

As we express our gratitude, we must never forget that the highest appreciation is not to utter words, but to live by them. – President John F. Kennedy

You get what you give. — Jennifer Lopez

If you look at what you have in life, you'll always have more. — Oprah Winfrey

Talent is God given. Be humble. Fame is man-given. Be grateful. Conceit is self-given. Be careful. — John Wooden

Chapter 10: Quotes About Character

Character is a key trait of great leaders. Many companies and organization espouse character, but it's not a universal trait of all leaders. This chapter contains quotes to fortify character.

To believe all men honest is folly. To believe none is something worse. — President John Adams

All men profess honesty as long as they can. To believe all men honest would be folly. To believe none so is something worse. — President John Quincy Adams

There is not respect for others without humility in one's self. — Henri Frederic Amiel

This is the very perfection of a man, to find out his own imperfection. — Saint Augustine

The first rule is to keep an untroubled spirit. The second is to look things in the face and know them for what they are. — Marcus Aurelius

Not everything that can be counted counts, and not everything that counts can be counted. — William Bruce Cameron

Show me the man you honor, and I will know what kind of man you are. — Thomas Carlisle

After I'm dead, I'd rather have people ask why I have no monument that way I have one. — Marcus Porcius Cato

Try to be like a turtle - at ease in your own shell. — Bill Copeland

Who sows virtue reaps honor. — Leonardo Da Vinci

I think you should take your job seriously, but not yourself. That is the best combination. — Dame Judi Dench

The supreme quality for leadership is unquestionably integrity. Without it, no real success is possible, no matter whether it is on a section gang, a football field, in an army, or in an office. — President Dwight D. Eisenhower

I believe fundamental honesty is the keystone of business. — Harvey S. Firestone

Quality means doing it right when no one is looking. — Henry Ford

Stop wearing your wishbone where your backbone ought to be. — Elizabeth Gilbert

The true test of character is to how much we know how to do, but how we behave when we don't know what to do. — John Holt

Any man worth his salt will stick up for what he believes right, but it takes a slightly better man to acknowledge instantly and without reservation that he is in error. — President Andrew Jackson

Whenever you do a thing, act as if all the world were watching. — President Thomas Jefferson

In matters of style, swim with the current. In matters of principle, stand like a rock. — President Thomas Jefferson

Doing what is right isn't the problem. It is knowing what is right. — Lyndon B. Johnson
 Wisdom is knowing what to do next, skill is knowing how to do it, and virtue is doing it. — David Star Jordan

There is one rule above all others, for being a man. Whatever comes, face it on your feet. — Robert Jordan

You take your life in your own hands, and what happens? A terrible thing: no one to blame. — Erica Jong

When your work speaks for itself, don't interrupt. — Henry J. Kaiser

Life's most persistent and urgent question is, 'What are you doing for others?' — Dr. Martin Luther King Jr.

Not everybody can be famous. But everybody can be great, because greatness is determined by service. — Dr. Martin Luther King Jr.

You are not only responsible for what you say, but also for what you do not say. — Dr. Martin Luther King Jr.

The time is always right to do the right thing. — Dr. Martin Luther King Jr.

The ultimate measure of a man is not where he stands in moments of comfort and convenience, but where he stands at times of challenge and uncertainty. — Dr. Martin Luther King Jr.

Talent is cheaper than table salt. What separates the talented individual from the successful one is a lot of hard work. — Stephen King

I cannot trust a man to control others who cannot control himself. — Robert E. Lee

You can tell the greatness of a man by what makes him angry. — President Abraham Lincoln

Nearly all men can stand adversity, but if you want to test a man's character, give him power. — President Abraham Lincoln

Character is like a tree and reputation like a shadow. The shadow is what we think of it; the tree is the real thing. — President Abraham Lincoln

You can fool all the people some of the time, and some of the people all the time, but you cannot fool all the people all the time. — President Abraham Lincoln

How many legs does a dog have if you call his tail a leg? Four. Saying that a tail is a leg doesn't make it a leg. — President Abraham Lincoln

Although you may spend your life killing, you will not exhaust all your foes. But if you quell your own anger your real enemy will be slain. — Akkineni Nagarjuna

To say you have no choice is to relieve yourself of responsibility. — Patrick Ness

When you see the right thing to do, you'd better do it. — Paul Newman

Treat people the way you want to be treated. Talk to people the way you want to be talked to. Respect is earned not given. — Hussein Nishah

Looking good isn't self-importance; it's self-respect. — Charles Nix

Character is how you treat those who can do nothing for you. — Al Pacino

Each person must live their life as a model for others. — Rosa Parks

Those who intend on becoming great should love neither themselves or their own things, but only what is just, whether it happens to be done by themselves or others. — Plato

The most important thing I learned is that soldiers watch what their leaders do. You can give them classes and lecture them forever, but it is your personal example they will follow. – General Colin Powell

It's your unlimited power to create and to love that can make the biggest difference in the quality of your life. — Tony Robbins

Courtesy is as much a mark of a gentleman as courage. — President Theodore Roosevelt

A man who is a master of patience is a master of everything else. — George Savile

Tough times never last, but tough people do. — Dr. Robert Schuller

Most powerful is he who has himself in his own power. — Seneca

How poor are they that have not patience! What wound did ever heal but by degrees? — William Shakespeare

This above all: to thine own self be true. – William Shakespeare

Don't hide your scars, they make you who you are.
— Frank Sinatra

The way to gain a good reputation Is to endeavor to be what you desire to appear. — Socrates

Respect for ourselves guides our morals, respect for others guides our manners. — Laurence Sterne

Be careful the environment you choose, for it will shape you; be careful the friends you choose, for you will be like them. — W. Clement Stone

I also have in mind that seemingly wealthy, but most terribly impoverished class of all, who have accumulated dross, but know not how to use it, or get rid of it, and thus have forged their own golden or silver fetters. — Henry David Thoreau

A man is only as good as his words are. — Rodd Thunderheart

Do not argue with an idiot. He will drag you down to his level and beat you with experience. — Mark Twain

It is better to keep your mouth closed and let people think you are a fool than to open it and remove all doubt. — Mark Twain

Popularity, I have always thought, may aptly be compared to a coquette - the more you woo her, the more apt is she to elude your embrace. — President John Tyler

It is easier to do a job right than to explain why you didn't. — President Martin Van Buren

Just try to be the best you can be; never cease trying to be the best you can be. That's in your power. — John Wooden

You can't let praise or criticism get to you. It's a weakness to get caught up in either one. — John Wooden

Be more concerned with your character than your reputation, because your character is what you really are, while your reputation is merely what others think you are. — John Wooden

The hero journey is inside of you; tear off the veils and open the mystery of yourself. — Malcolm X

Chapter 11: Quotes About Creativity

Leaders have several roles. They are the captain, the mentor, the coach, the manager and more. Creativity is critical for solving problems. The problems can be issues facing the business or even the development of people. Creativity helps leaders identify connections that others may not see and to create options others may not consider. This chapter highlights the importance of creativity.

Ideas are the only things I can change the world. The rest is details. — Scott Adams

Circumstances, what are circumstances? I make circumstances. — Napoléon Bonaparte

A problem clearly stated is a problem half solved. — Dorthea Brande

Unless you dream, you're not going to achieve anything. — Sir Richard Branson

Perfection is not when there is no more to add, but no more to take away. — Antoine De Saint-Exupery

We keep moving forward, opening new doors, and doing new things, because we're curious and curiosity keeps leading us down new paths. — Walt Disney

Reading, after a certain age, diverts the mind too much from its creative pursuits. Any man who reads too much and uses his own brain too little falls into lazy habits of thinking. — Albert Einstein

Logic will get you from A to B. Imagination will take you everywhere. — Albert Einstein

Don't find fault, find a remedy. — Henry Ford

Ideas control the world. — President James A. Garfield

Life's like a movie; write your won ending, keep believing, keep pretending. — Jim Henson

Wonder rather than doubt is the root of all knowledge. — Abraham Joshua Heschel

Never limit yourself because of others' limited imagination; never limit others because of your own limited imagination. — Mae Jemison

You have to be burning with an idea, or a problem, or a wrong that you want to right. If you're not passionate enough from the start, you'll never stick it out. — Steve Jobs

Obstacles don't have to stop you. If you run into a wall, dot turn around and give up. Figure out how to climb it, go through it, or work around it. — Michael Jordan

There exist limitless opportunities in every industry. Where there is an open mind, there will always be a frontier. — Charles Kettering

Ideas shape the course of history. — John Maynard Keynes

Limitations live only in our minds. But if we use our imaginations, our possibilities become limitless. — Jamie Paolinetti

A creative man is motivated by the desire to achieve, not the desire to beat others. — Ayn Rand

Without leaps of imagination, or dreaming, we lose the excitement of possibilities. Dreaming, after all, is a form of planning. — Gloria Steinem

The things we fear most in organizations--fluctuations, disturbances, imbalances--are the primary sources of creativity. — Margaret Wheatley

Chapter 12: Quotes About Innovation

Innovation is important. It's the fuel that solves problems. It influences the culture of an organization and it can change the trajectory of careers and companies. This chapter contains quotes about innovation and creativity.

The manager accepts the status quo; the leader challenges it. — Warren Bennis

There are two ways of being creative. One can sing and dance. Or one can create an environment in which singers and dancers flourish. — Warren Bennis

In life, change is inevitable. In business, change is vital. — Warren Bennis

Embrace what you don't know, especially in the beginning, because what you don't know can become your greatest asset. It ensures that you will absolutely be doing things different from everybody else. — Sara Blakely

As you start your journey, the first thing you should do is throw away that store-bought map and begin to draw your own. — Michael Dell

People in any organization are always attached to the obsolete - the things that should have worked but did not, the things that once were productive and no longer are. — Peter F. Drucker

Out of clutter, find simplicity. From discord, find harmony. In the middle of difficulty lies opportunity. — Albert Einstein

Do not go where the path may lead, go instead where there is no path and leave a trail. — Ralph Waldo Emerson

The man who will use his skill and constructive imagination to see how much he can give for a dollar, instead of how little he can give for a dollar, is bound to succeed. — Henry Ford

Opportunities don't happen. You create them. — Chris Grosser

When you find an idea that you just can't stop thinking about, that's probably a good one to pursue. — Josh James

Innovation distinguishes between a leader and a follower. — Steve Jobs

Conformity is the jailer of freedom and the enemy of growth. — President John F. Kennedy

Change is the law of life. And those who look only to the past or present are certain to miss the future. – President John F. Kennedy

The trouble in America is not that we are making too many mistakes, but that we are making too few. — Phillip Knight

It must be remembered that there is nothing more difficult to plan, more doubtful of success, nor more dangerous to manage than a new system. For the initiator has the enmity of all who would profit by the preservation of the old institution and merely lukewarm defenders in those who gain by the new ones. — Niccolò Machiavelli

Do not follow where the path may lead. Go instead where there is no path and leave a trail. — Harold R. McAlindon

It is better to fail in originality than to succeed in imitation. — Herman Melville

Even if you're on the right track, you'll get run over if you just sit there. — Will Rogers

We learn wisdom from failure much more than from success; we often discover what will do, by finding out what will not do; and probably he who never made a mistake never made a discovery. — Samuel Smiles

Whenever you find yourself on the side of the majority, it is time to pause and reflect. — Mark Twain

Chapter 13 Quotes About Engagement

Engagement is a very hot topic. Thought leaders like Simon Sinek, Dan Pink, Marcus Buckingham and Chester Elton have written extensively on the topic. They demonstrate that engaged employees are more loyal and more productive.

This chapter has quotes about the role of engaging employees and about how to do it.

Everyone talks about building a relationship with your customer. I think you build one with your employees first. — Angela Ahrendts

I've learned that people will forget what you said, people will forget what you did, but people will never forget how you made them feel. — Maya Angelou

Pleasure in the job puts perfection in the work. — Aristotle

Pretend every single person you meet has a sign around their neck that says, "make me feel important." Not only will you succeed in sales, you will succeed in life. — Mary Kay Ash

We treat our people like royalty. If you honor and serve the people who work for you, they will honor and serve you. — Mary Kay Ash

There are two things people want more than sex and money: recognition and praise. — Mary Kay Ash

People forget years and remember moments. — Ann Beattie

One of the best ways to influence people is to make them feel important. — Roy T. Bennett

Trust is the lubrication that makes it possible for the organization to work. — Warren Bennis

Good leaders make people feel that they're at the very heart of things, not at the periphery. — Warren Bennis

Too many companies believe people are interchangeable. Truly gifted people never are. They have unique talents. Such people cannot be forced into roles they are not suited for, nor should they be. Effective leaders allow great people to do the work they were born to do. — Warren Bennis

Highly engaged employees make the customer experience. Disengaged employees break it. — Timothy R. Clark

No man ever listened himself out of a job. — President Calvin Coolidge

Always treat your employees exactly as you want them to treat your best customers. — Stephen Covey

When people talk, listen completely. — Ernest Hemingway

Dispirited, unmotivated, unappreciated workers cannot compete in a highly competitive world. — Frances Hesselbein

Everyone enjoys doing the kind of work for which he is best suited. — Napoleon Hill

Your number one customers are your people. Look after employees first and then customers last. — Ian Hutchinson

I love what I do, and when you love what you do, you want to be the best at it. — Jay-Z

We have but two ears and one mouth, so that we may listen twice as much as we speak. — President Thomas Jefferson

Listening is an art that requires attention over talent, spirit over ego, others over self. — Dean Johnson

Make people feel like the hero of their journey and they will do more. — Maxime Lagacé

We meet no ordinary people in our lives. — C. S. Lewis

Tact is the ability to describe others as they see themselves. — President Abraham Lincoln

Everyone sees what you appear to be, few experience what you really are. — Niccolò Machiavelli

There is no other way to guard yourself against flattery than by making men understand that telling you the truth will not offend you. — Niccolò Machiavelli

Men are driven by two principal impulses, either by love or by fear. — Niccolò Machiavelli

Beginning today, treat everyone you meet as if they were going to be dead by midnight. Extend to them all the care, kindness and understanding you can muster, and do it with no thought of any reward. Your life will never be the same again. — Og Mandingo

There is no investment you can make which will pay you so well as the effort to scatter sunshine and good cheer through your establishment. — Orison Swett Marden

Tend to the people, and they will tend to the business. — John C. Maxwell

One bad day from one member of my staff doesn't mean they are not really good at their jobs the rest of the time. I play a long game in terms of management. — Helen McCabe

One of the most sincere forms of respect is actually listening to what another has to say. — Bryant H. McGill

Following is one of the most underrated aspects of leadership. I have seen many a good [military unit] underachieve because someone...thought the commander was incompetent, and quietly worked to undermine his authority. — Admiral William McRaven

Never tell people how to do things. Tell them what to do and they will surprise you with their ingenuity. — General George S. Patton

Inventories can be managed, but people must be led. — H. Ross Perot

All employees have an innate desire to contribute to something bigger than themselves. — Jag Randhawa

You take people as far as they will go, not as far as you would like them to go. — Jeanette Rankin

What I have learned is that people become motivated when you guide them to the source of their own power and when you make heroes out of employees who personify what you want to see in the organization. — Anita Roddick

The best executive is the one who has sense enough to pick good men to do what he wants done, and self-restraint to keep from meddling with them while they do it. — President Theodore Roosevelt

Motivation comes from working on things we care about. — Sheryl Sandberg

I consider my ability to arouse enthusiasm among men the greatest asset I possess. The way to develop the best that is in a man is by appreciation and encouragement. — Charles M. Schwab

The truth of the matter is that you always know the right thing to do. The hard part is doing it. — General Norman Schwarzkopf

He who has great power should use it lightly. — Seneca

People don't buy what you do, they buy why you do it. — Simon Sinek

When people are financially invested, they want a return. When people are emotionally invested, they want to contribute. — Simon Sinek

The way your employees feel is the way your customers will feel. And if your employees don't feel valued, neither will your customers. — Sybil F. Stershic

Culture is about performance, and making people feel good about how they contribute to the whole. — Tracy Streckenbach

Keep away from people who try to belittle your ambitions. Small people always do that, but the really great make you feel that you, too, can become great. — Mark Twain

A leader is best when people barely know he exists. When his work is done, his aim fulfilled, they will all say: We did it ourselves. — Lao Tzu

Most men are not scolded out of their opinion. — President Martin Van Buren

Treat people as if they were what they ought to be, and you help them become what they are capable of being. — Johann Wolfgang von Goethe

Outstanding leaders go out of their way to boost the self-confidence of their personnel. If people believe in themselves, it's amazing what they can accomplish. — Sam Walton

When we seek to discover the best in others, we somehow bring out the best in ourselves. — William Arthur Ward

The ear of the leader must ring with the voices of the people. — President Woodrow Wilson

Chapter 14: Quotes About Courage

All great leaders must demonstrate courage. Each day leaders must make decisions about their business, it's culture and it's people. Many of these decisions are difficult with no clear "right" answer. Leaders be courageous enough to make tough decisions, communicate them, and navigate the consequences.

This chapter contains quotes about courage. This is an inspiring chapter!

Courage and perseverance have a magical talisman, before which difficulties disappear, and obstacles vanish into air. — President John Quincy Adams

Everything you've always wanted is on the other side of fear. — George Addair

If the highest aim of a captain were to preserve his ship, he would keep it in port forever. — Saint Thomas Aquinas

There is only one way to avoid criticism: do nothing, say nothing and be nothing. — Aristotle

Courage isn't having the strength to go on - it is going on when you don't have strength. — Napoléon Bonaparte

Too many of us are not living our dreams because we're living our fears. — Les Brown

The cave you fear to enter holds the treasure you seek. — Joseph Campbell

The most courageous act is still to think for yourself. Aloud. — Coco Chanel

The hardest thing to do is to be true to yourself, especially when everybody is watching. — Dave Chappelle

Success is not final; failure is not fatal; it is the courage to continue that counts. — Winston Churchill

A man does what he must - in spite of personal consequences, in spite of obstacles and dangers and pressures — and that is the basis of all human morality. — Winston Churchill

Courage is what it takes to stand up and speak. Courage is also what it takes to sit down and listen. — Winston Churchill

Courage is the first of human qualities because it is the quality which guarantees all others. — Winston Churchill

All our dreams can come true if we have the courage to pursue them. — Walt Disney

Whenever you see a successful business, someone once made a courageous decision. — Peter F. Drucker

People who don't take risks generally make about two big mistakes a year. People who do take risks generally make about two big mistakes a year. — Peter F. Drucker

Worry retards reaction and makes clear-cut decisions impossible. — Amelia Earhart

Courage is the price that life exacts for granting peace, the soul that knows it not, knows no release from little things. — Amelia Earhart

A person who never made a mistake never tried anything new. — Albert Einstein

Great spirits have always found violent opposition from mediocrities. The latter cannot understand it when a man does not thoughtlessly submit to hereditary prejudices but honestly and courageously uses his intelligence. — Albert Einstein

Only those who will risk going too far can possibly find out how far one can go. — T. S. Eliot

To be yourself in a world that is constantly trying to make you something else is the greatest accomplishment. — Ralph Waldo Emerson

The important thing is not being afraid to take a chance. Remember, the greatest failure is to not try. Once you find something you love to do, be the best at doing it. — Debbi Fields

Two roads diverged in the wood, and I - I took the one less traveled by, and that has made all the difference. — Robert Frost

The most confident critics are generally those who know the least about the matter criticized. — President Ulysses S. Grant

You miss 100% of the shots you don't take. — Wayne Gretzky

Great deeds are usually wrought at great risks. — Herodotus

The number one reason people fail in life is because they listen to their friends, family members and neighbors. — Napoleon Hill

Fearlessness is like a muscle. I know from my own life that the more I exercise it, the more natural it becomes not to let my fears run me. — Arianna Huffington

The rung of a ladder was never meant to rest upon, but only to hold a man's foot long enough to enable him to put the other somewhat higher. — Thomas Huxley

Surviving a failure gives you more self-confidence. Failures are a great learning tools...but they must be kept to a minimum. — Jeffrey Immelt

Be not afraid of life. Believe that it is worth living, and your belief will help create the fact. — William James

Have the courage to follow your heart and intuition. They somehow know what you truly want to become. — Steve Jobs

What would you do if you weren't afraid? — Spencer Johnson

If you accept the expectations of others, especially negative ones, then you never will change the outcome. — Michael Jordan

Live daringly, boldly, fearlessly. Taste the relish to be found in competition - inhaling put forth the best within you. — Henry J. Kaiser

Never bend your head. Always hold it high. Look the world straight in the eye. — Helen Keller

There are risks and costs to action. But they are far less than the long-range risks of comfortable inaction. — President John F. Kennedy

Believe and act as if it were impossible to fail. — Charles Kettering

The time is always right to do the right thing. — Dr. Martin Luther King Jr.

The scariest moment is always just before you start. — Stephen King

If you can you should, and if you're brave enough to start, you will. — Stephen King

The only real prison is fear and the only real freedom is freedom from fear. — Aung San Suu Kyi

The difference between a successful person and others is not a lack of strength, not a lack of knowledge, but rather a lack of will. — Vince Lombardi

A man who wants to lead the orchestra must turn his back on the crowd. — Max Lucado

A true leader has the confidence to stand alone, the courage to make tough decisions, and the compassion to listen to the needs of others. He does not set out to be a leader but becomes one by the equality of his actions and the integrity of his intent. — General Douglas MacArthur

Never was anything great achieved without danger. — Niccolò Machiavelli

All courses of action are risky, so prudence is not in avoiding danger (it's impossible), but in calculating risk and acting decisively. Make mistakes of ambition and not mistakes of sloth. Develop the strength to do bold things, not the strength to suffer. — Niccolò Machiavelli

I learned that courage was not the absence of fear, but the triumph over it. The brave man is not he who does not feel afraid, but he who conquers that fear. — Nelson Mandela

Truth uncompromisingly told will always have its jagged edges. — Herman Melville

Take chances, make mistakes. That's how you grow. Pain nourishes your courage. You have to fail in order to practice being brave. — Mary Tyler Moore

There is a tremendous bias against taking risks. Everyone is trying to optimize their ass-covering. — Elon Musk

All you need is the plan, the road map and the courage to press on to your destination. — Earl Nightingale

You are only as good as the chances you take. — Al Pacino

I have learned over the years that when one's mind is made up, this diminishes fear; knowing what must be done does away with fear. — Rosa Parks

Courage is knowing what not to fear. — Plato

We can easily forgive a child who is afraid of the dark; the real tragedy of life is when men are afraid of the light. — Plato

The future doesn't belong to the fainthearted; it belongs to the brave. — President Ronald Reagan

I live my life through freak. If I'm afraid of it, I'll do it just so I'm not afraid of it anymore. — Jeremy Renner

You gain strength, courage and confidence by every experience in which you really stop to look fear in the face. You must do the thing you think you cannot do. — Eleanor Roosevelt

It is hard to fail, but it is worse never to have tried to succeed. — President Theodore Roosevelt

It takes a great deal of courage to stand up to your enemies, but even more to stand up to your friends. — J. K. Rowling

What great thing would you attempt if you know you could not fail? — Dr. Robert Schuller

We suffer more in imagination than in reality. — Seneca

The bravest sight in the world is to see a great man struggling against adversity. — Seneca

Our doubts are traitors and make us lose the good we oft might win by fearing to attempt. — William Shakespeare

Be not afraid of greatness; some are born great, some achieve greatness, and others have greatness thrust upon them. — William Shakespeare

A ship in harbor is safe, but that is not what ships are built for. — John A. Shedd

Though no one can go back and make a brand new start, anyone can start from now and make a brand new ending. — James R. Sherman, Ph. D.

Falling down is not a failure. Failure comes when you stay where you have fallen. — Socrates

Keep your fears to yourself but share your courage with others. — Robert Louis Stevenson

Great things never come from comfort zones. — Neil Strauss

Giving up doesn't always mean you're weak. Sometimes you're just strong enough to let go. — Taylor Swift

Anyone can hold the helm when the sea is calm. — Publilius Syrus

Only those who risk going too far can possibly find out how far one can go. — Eric Thomas, Ph. D.

Criticism is easier to take when you realize that the only people who aren't criticized are those who don't take risks. —President Donald J. Trump

Twenty years from now you will be more disappointed by the things you didn't' do than by the ones you did do, so throw off the bow lines, sail away from safe harbor, catch the Tradewinds in your sails. Explore. Dream. Discover. — Mark Twain

Care about what other people think and you'll always be their prisoner. — Lao Tzu

Life begins at the end of your comfort zone. — Neal Donald Walsch

If you want to make enemies, try to change something. — President Woodrow Wilson

Success is never final; failure is never fatal. It's courage that counts. — John Wooden

Success is peace of mind, which is a direct result of self-satisfaction in knowing you made the effort to become the best of which you are capable. — John Wooden

Adversity is the state in which man most easily becomes acquainted with himself, being especially free of admirers then. — John Wooden

Named must your fear be before banish it you can.
— Yoda

Be who you are and say what you feel, because those who mind don't matter and those who matter don't mind. — Sir Mark A. Young

Do not be distracted by criticism. Remember the only taste of success some people get is to take a bite out of you. — Zig Ziglar

One of the main reasons people fail to reach their full potential is because they are unwilling to risk anything. — Zig Ziglar

Chapter 15: Quotes About Kindness

You could argue that the quotes in this chapter could have been lumped together with the chapter on engagement. Demonstrating kindness demonstrates caring and people we lead are more engaged when we know we care.

I called out this virtue as independent from engagement because it deserves a place of it's own in the leader's mind. Author Traivs Bradberry said it well when he wrote of balancing between being genuinely kind, and not looking weak.

Th quotes in this section may inspire you to consider your view of how kindness fits into a leader's world and how you can demonstrate kindness consistently across your team and your organization.

Remember there's no such thing as a small act of kindness. Every act creates a ripple with no logical end. — Scott Adams

No act of kindness, no matter how small is ever wasted. — Aesop

Never leave a good act undone just because it's small. — Liu Bei

One of the toughest things for leaders to master is kindness. Kindness shares credit and offers enthusiastic praise for others' work. It's a balancing act between being genuinely kind and not looking weak. — Travis Bradberry

Choose being kind over being right and you'll be right every time. — Richard Carlson

You have it easily in your power to increase the sum total of this world's happiness now. How? By giving a few words of sincere appreciation to someone who is lonely or discouraged. Perhaps you will forget tomorrow the kind words you say today, but the recipient may cherish them over a lifetime. — Dale Carnegie

Don't criticize what you can't understand. — Bob Dylan

A single act of kindness throws out roots in all directions, and the roots spring up and make new trees. — Amelia Earhart

You cannot do a kindness too soon, for you never know how soon it will be too late. — Ralph Waldo Emerson

Forgiveness is not an occasional act; it is a permanent attitude. — Dr. Martin Luther King Jr.

Be kind whenever possible. It is always possible. — Dalai Lama

Do I not destroy my enemies when I make them my friends? — President Abraham Lincoln

Be kind for everyone you meet is fighting a hard battle. — Ian MacLaren

Kind words are short and easy to speak, but their echoes are truly endless. — Mother Teresa

I have found that if you love life, life will love you back. — Arthur Rubinstein

I have three precious things which I hold fast and prize. The first is gentleness; the second is frugality; the third is humility, which keeps me from putting myself before others. Be gentle and you can be bold; be frugal and you can be liberal; avoid putting yourself before others and you can become a leader among men. — Lao Tzu

Most men are not scolded out of their opinion. — President Martin Van Buren

If you want to lift yourself up, lift up someone else. — Booker T. Washington

As a general rule, it pays to be confident, helpful and nice. — Colin Wright

Chapter 16: Quotes About Growth and Development

Great leaders develop their people. The encourage, prod and challenge their direct reports to do more than they themselves believe they are capable of doing.

The quotes in this chapter are all about growth and development. They're about setting expectations and guiding people to be their best. Read on...

From a small seed a mighty trunk may grow. — Aeschylus

God loves to help him who strives to help himself. — Aeschylus

Painful as it may be, a significant emotional event can be the catalyst for choosing a direction that serves us - and those around us - more effectively. Look for the learning. — Louisa May Alcott

Nothing will work unless you do. — Maya Angelou

Let the improvement of yourself keep you so busy that you have no time to criticize others. — Roy T. Bennett

Leaders should always expect the very best of those around them. They know that people can change and grow. — Warren Bennis

Excellence is a better teacher than mediocrity. The lessons of the ordinary are everywhere. Truly profound and original insights are to be found only in studying the exemplary. — Warren Bennis

If everything was perfect, you would never learn, and you would never grow — Beyoncé

Remember, feedback is meant to address the problem, not the person. — Travis Bradberry

Follow your bliss and the universe will open doors where there were only walls. — Joseph Campbell

If you fear making anyone mad, then you ultimately probe for the lowest common denominator of human achievement. — President Jimmy Carter

Mountaintops inspire leaders but valleys mature them. — Winston Churchill

All growth depends on activity. There is no development physically or intellectually without effort, and effort means work. — President Calvin Coolidge

Death is not the greatest loss in life. The greatest loss is what dies inside us while we live. — Norman Cousins

Be patient with yourself. Self-growth is tender; its holy ground. There is no greater investment. — Stephen Covey

Celebrate the effort, for it is in the trying that you discover you. — Sima Dahl

Learning never exhausts the mind. — Leonardo Da Vinci

In the end, it is important to remember that we cannot become what we need to be by remaining what we are. — Max De Pree

It is the capacity to develop and improve their skills that distinguishes leaders from followers. — Peter F. Drucker

Opportunity is missed by most people because it is dressed in overalls and looks like work. — Thomas A. Edison

It's never too late to be what you might have been. — George Elliott

Always dream and shoot higher than you know you can do. Don't bother just to be better than your contemporaries or predecessors. Try to be better than yourself. — William Faulkner

Life is a series of experiences, each one of which makes us bigger, even though sometimes it is hard to realize this. For the world was built to develop character, and we must learn that the setbacks and grieves which we endure help us in our marching onward. — Henry Ford

Tell me and I forget. Teach me and I remember. Involve me and I learn. — Benjamin Franklin

One day, in retrospect, the years of struggle will strike you as the most beautiful. — Sigmund Freud

Today a reader, tomorrow a leader. — Margaret Fuller

Strength does not come from winning. Your struggles develop your strengths. — Mahatma Gandhi

Your most unhappy customers are your greatest source of learning. — Bill Gates

Kick your own ass first. — Jeffrey Gitomer

If it scares you, it might be a good thing to try. — Seth Godin

The miracle is not to walk on water. The miracle is to walk on the green earth, dwelling deeply in the present moment and feeling truly alive. — Thich Nhat Hahn

No man ever steps in the same river twice, for it's not the same river and he's not the same man. — Heraclitus

The wise know their weakness too well to assume infallibility; and he who knows most, knows best how little he knows. — President Thomas Jefferson

Good, better, best. Never let it rest 'til your good is better and your better is best. — St. Jerome

You aren't learning anything when you're talking. — President Lyndon B. Johnson

Those who spend their time looking for the faults in others usually make no time to correct their own. — Art Jonak

Only those who are asleep make no mistakes. — Ingvar Kamprad

Leadership and learning are indispensable to each other. — President John F. Kennedy

Even if I knew that tomorrow the world would go to pieces, I would still plant my apple tree. — Dr. Martin Luther King Jr.

In the real world, the smartest people are people who make mistakes and learn. In school, the smartest people don't make mistakes. — Robert Kiyosaki

When you talk, you are only repeating what you already know. But if you listen, you may learn something new. — Dalai Lama

Books serve to show a man that those original thoughts of his aren't very new at all. — President Abraham Lincoln

Education begins the gentleman, but reading, good company and reflection must finish him. — John Locke

A man who is used to acting in one way never changes; he must come to ruin when the times, in changing are no longer in harmony with his ways. — Niccolò Machiavelli

A prudent man should always follow in the path trodden by great men and imitate those who are most excellent, so that if he does not attain to their greatness, at any rate he will get some tinge of it. — Niccolò Machiavelli

Knowledge will forever govern ignorance, and a people who mean to be their own governors, must arm themselves with the power knowledge gives. — President James Madison

You can't knock on opportunity's door and not be ready. — Bruno Mars

Be so good they can't ignore you. — Steve Martin

Be willing to be uncomfortable. Be comfortable being uncomfortable. It may get tough, but it's a small price to pay for living a dream. — Peter McWilliams

We are all ordinary. We are all boring. We are all spectacular. We are all shy. We are all bold. We are all heroes. We are all helpless. It just depends on the day. — Brad Meltzer

I am still learning. — Michelangelo

You're not going to get very far in life based on what you already know. You're going to advance in life by what you're going to learn after you leave here. — Charlie Munger

Change will not come if we wait for some other person or some other time. We are the one's we've been waiting for. We are the change we seek. — President Barack H. Obama

If you don't like the road you're walking on, start paving another one. — Dolly Parton

People are like dirt. They can either nourish you and help you grow as a person or they can stunt your growth and make you wilt and die. — Plato

Know how to listen and you will profit even from those who talk badly. — Plutarch

Good judgement comes from experience, and a lot of that comes from bad judgement. — Will Rogers

A formal education will make you a living; self-education will make you a fortune. — Jim Rohn

Things don't get better until you get better. — Jim Rohn

Instead of looking at the past, I put myself ahead 20 years and try to look at what I need to do now in order to get there then — Diana Ross

No man was ever wise by chance — Seneca

Associate with people who are likely to improve you. — Seneca

Life isn't about finding yourself. Life is about creating yourself. — George Bernard Shaw

Don't judge each day by the harvest you reap, but by the seeds you plant. — Robert Louis Stevenson

Everyone thinks of changing the world, but no one thinks of changing himself. — Leo Tolstoy

The mediocre teacher tells. The good teacher explains. The superior teacher demonstrates. The great teacher inspires. — William Arthur Ward

The greatest crime in the world is not developing your potential. When you do what you do best, you are helping not only yourself but the world. — Roger Williams

The best competition I have is against myself to become better. — John Wooden

What you get by achieving your goals is not as important as what you come by
achieving your goals. — Zig Ziglar

Chapter 17 Quotes About Teamwork

All great leaders are part of a team whether the are part of the senior most leadership in the company or a sales representative running their sales territory.

In most situations, leaders know that without teamwork, their plans will not be executed and the goals of the team or organization will not be met.

Enjoy the quotes in this section. They highlight the importance of teamwork.

It takes two flints to make a fire. — Louisa May Alcott

Don't let winning make you soft. Don't let losing make you quiet. Don't let your teammates down in any situation. — Larry Bird

Thousands of candles can be lighted from a single candle. Happiness never decreases by being shared. — Buddha

Coming together is a beginning; keeping together is progress; working together is success. — Henry Ford

If everyone is moving forward together, then success takes care of itself. — Henry Ford

The strength of the team is each member. The strength of each member is the team. — Phil Jackson

There are no problems we cannot solve together, and very few that we can solve by ourselves. — President Lyndon B. Johnson

Talent wins games, but teamwork and intelligence wins championships. — Michael Jordan

Alone we can do so little; together we can do so much. — Helen Keller

Great teams do not hold back with one another. They are unafraid to air their dirty laundry. They admit their mistakes, their weaknesses, and their concerns without fear of reprisal. — Patrick Lencioni

No one can whistle a symphony. It takes a while whole orchestra to play it. —H.E. Luccock

Teamwork makes the dream work. — John C. Maxwell

Individually, we are one drop. Together, we are an ocean. — Ryunosuke Satoro

Success is empty if you arrive at the finish line alone. The best reward is to get there surrounded by winners. — Howard Schultz

Whatever you do in life, surround yourself with smart people who'll argue with you. — John Wooden

The main ingredient of stardom is the rest of the team. — John Wooden

Section 2: Quotes by Person

President John Adams, US President (1797-1801)
To believe all men honest is folly. To believe none is something worse.

President John Quincy Adams, US President (1817-1825)
If your actions inspire others to dream more, learn more, do more and become more, you are a leader.

All men profess honesty as long as they can. To believe all men honest would be folly. To believe none so is something worse.

Courage and perseverance have a magical talisman, before which difficulties disappear, and obstacles vanish into air.

Scott Adams, Author, entrepreneur, keynote speaker, creator of the Dilbert comic strip
Ideas are the only things I can change the world. The rest is details.

Remember there's no such thing as a small act of kindness. Every act creates a ripple with no logical end.

George Addair, Speaker, philosopher and author
Everything you've always wanted is on the other side of fear.

Aeschylus, Ancient Greek tragedian
From a small seed a mighty trunk may grow

God loves to help him who strives to help himself.

Aesop, Greek fabulist and storyteller
No act of kindness, no matter how small is ever wasted.

Angela Ahrendts, American businesswoman
Everyone talks about building a relationship with your customer. I think you build one with your employees first.

Louisa May Alcott, American novelist, short story writer and poet
He who believes is strong; he who doubts is weak. Strong convictions precede great actions.

We all have our own life to pursue, our own kind of dream to be weaving, and we all have the power to make wishes come true, as long as we keep believing.

Do the things you know, and you shall learn the truth you need to know

Painful as it may be, a significant emotional event can be the catalyst for choosing a direction that serves us - and those around us - more effectively. Look for the learning.

It takes two flints to make a fire.

Alexander the Great, Ancient Greek King of Macedon, member of the Argead dynasty
There is nothing impossible to him who will try.

I am not afraid of an army of lions led by a sheep.
I am afraid of an army of sheep led by a lion.

Muhammad Ali, American professional boxing World Champion, activist, and philanthropist
I am the greatest. I said that even before I knew I was.

Michael Altshuler, American businessman, speaker, and consultant
The bad news is time flies. The good news is you're the pilot.

Henri Frederic Amiel, Swiss moral philosopher, poet, and critic
There is not respect for others without humility in one's self.

Mario Andretti, Italian-born American former racing driver
If everything seems under control, you're not going fast enough.

Maya Angelou, American poet, singer, memoirist, and civil rights activist
Try to be a rainbow in someone else's cloud.

Nothing can dim the light that shines from within.

Nothing will work unless you do.

I've learned that you shouldn't go through life with a catcher's mitt on both hands; you need to be able to throw something back.

I've learned that people will forget what you said, people will forget what you did, but people will never forget how you made them feel.

Nothing will work unless you do.

Susan B. Anthony, American social reformer and women's rights activist
Nothing is hopeless that is right.

Antiochus, Hellenistic king of the Seleucid Empire
Our greatest glory is not in never failing, but in rising every time we fail.

Saint Thomas Aquinas, Italian Dominican friar, philosopher, Catholic priest, and Doctor of the Church
If the highest aim of a captain were to preserve his ship, he would keep it in port forever.

Archilochus, Greek lyric poet
We don't rise to the level of our expectations; we fall to the level of our training.

Aristotle, Greek philosopher
He who cannot be a good follower cannot be a good leader.

Quality is not an act; it is a habit.

We are what we repeatedly do. Excellence, then, is not an act, but a habit.

What it lies in our power to do, it lies in our power not to do.

Pleasure in the job puts perfection in the work.

There is only one way to avoid criticism: do nothing, say nothing and be nothing.

M. D. Arnold, Author
A good leader leads the people from above them. A great leader leads the people from within them.

Mary Kay Ash, American businesswoman
The greatest pollution problem we face today is negativity. Eliminate the negative attitude and believe you can do anything.

Don't let the negatives of life control you. Rise above them. Use them as your steppingstones to go higher than you ever dreamed possible.

For every failure there's an alternative course of action. you just have to find it.

Pretend every single person you meet has a sign around their neck that says, "make me feel important." Not only will you succeed in sales, you will succeed in life.

We treat our people like royalty. If you honor and serve the people who work for you, they will honor and serve you.

There are two things people want more than sex and money: recognition and praise.

Arthur Ashe, American professional tennis player
From what we get, we can make a living, what we give, however, makes a life.

St. Francis of Assisi, Italian Catholic friar, deacon and preacher
Start by doing what's necessary; then do what's possible; and suddenly you're doing the impossible.

Francis Atterbury, English man of letters, politician and bishop
It's attention to detail that make the difference between average and stunning.

Saint Augustine, Catholic bishop and theologian, Roman African, doctor of the Church, and Neoplatonic philosopher
This is the very perfection of a man, to find out his own imperfection.

Marcus Aurelius, Roman emperor from 161 to 180 and a Stoic philosopher

In your actions, don't procrastinate. In your conversations, don't confuse. In your thoughts, don't wander. In your soul, don't be passive or aggressive. In your life, don't be all about business.

You have power over your mind – not outside events. Realize this, and you will find strength.

A man's life is what his thoughts make of it.

Everything we hear is an opinion, not a fact. Everything we see is a perspective, not the truth.

What we do now echoes in eternity.

Do not indulge in dreams of having what you have not, but recon up the chief of the blessings you do possess, and then thankfully remember how you would crave for them if they were not yours.

The first rule is to keep an untroubled spirit. The second is to look things in the face and know them for what they are.

Richard Bach, American writer

The more I want to get something done, the less I call it work. — Richard Bach

Arthur Balfour, 1st Earl of Balfour, British Statesman, Former Prime Minister of the United Kingdom (1902 - 1905)
Enthusiasm moves the world.

Joel Barker, Technology and business futurist, author
A leader is a person you will follow to a place you would not go by yourself.

Ann Beattie, American novelist and short story writer
People forget years and remember moments.

Liu Bei, Chinese warlord in the late Eastern Han dynasty
Never leave a good act undone just because it's small.

Alexander Graham Bell, Scottish-born American inventor, scientist, and engineer
The achievement of one goal should be the starting point of another.

When one door closes another one opens; but we so often look so long and so regretfully upon the closed door, that we do not see the ones which open for us

Concentrate all your thoughts upon the work in hand. The sun's rays do not burn until brought to a focus.

Roy T. Bennett, Author
The key to successful leadership is influence, not authority.

One of the best ways to influence people is to make them feel important.

Let the improvement of yourself keep you so busy that you have no time to criticize others.

Warren Bennis, Organizational consultant and Author
Leadership is the capacity to translate vision into reality.

The manager asks how and when; the leader asks what and why.

Good leaders make people feel that they're at the very heart of things, not at the periphery.

Becoming a leader is synonymous with becoming yourself. It is precisely that simple and it is also that difficult.

Leaders are people who believe so passionately that they can seduce other people into sharing their dream.

Failing organizations are usually over-managed and under-led.

Success in management requires learning as fast as the world is changing.

The manager accepts the status quo; the leader challenges it.

There are two ways of being creative. One can sing and dance. Or one can create an environment in which singers and dancers flourish.

In life, change is inevitable. In business, change is vital.

Trust is the lubrication that makes it possible for the organization to work.

Good leaders make people feel that they're at the very heart of things, not at the periphery.

Too many companies believe people are interchangeable. Truly gifted people never are. They have unique talents. Such people cannot be forced into roles they are not suited for, nor should they be. Effective leaders allow great people to do the work they were born to do.

Leaders should always expect the very best of those around them. They know that people can change and grow.

Excellence is a better teacher than mediocrity. The lessons of the ordinary are everywhere. Truly profound and original insights are to be found only in studying the exemplary.

Henri Bergson, French philosopher
Think like a man of action, act like a man of thought.

Yogi Berra, American professional baseball player, coach, and manager
If you don't set goals, you can't regret not reaching them.

Beyoncé, American singer, songwriter, record producer, dancer and actress
If everything was perfect, you would never learn, and you would never grow.

Jeff Bezos, American businessman, media proprietor, and investor
I knew that if I failed I wouldn't regret that, but I knew the one thing I might regret is not trying.

Larry Bird, American former professional basketball player, coach and executive in the National Basketball Association
Don't let winning make you soft. Don't let losing make you quiet. Don't let your teammates down in any situation.

Tony Blair, Former British Prime Minister (1997-2007)
The art of leadership is saying no, not saying yes. It is very easy to say yes.

Sara Blakely, American businesswoman, entrepreneur, and philanthropist

Embrace what you don't know, especially in the beginning, because what you don't know can become your greatest asset. It ensures that you will absolutely be doing things different from everybody else.

Ken Blanchard, Author, management trainer and consultant

Servant-leadership is all about making the goals clear and then rolling your sleeves up and doing whatever it takes to help people win. In that situation, they don't work for you, you work for them.

The greatest leaders mobilize others by coalescing people around a shared vision.

Connect the dots between individual roles and the goals of the organization. When people see that connection, they get a lot of energy out of work. They feel the importance, dignity, and meaning in their job.

The key to successful leadership is influence, not authority.

Niels Bohr, Danish physicist, Nobel Prize in Physics

An expert is a person who has made all the mistakes that can be made in a very narrow field.

Napoléon Bonaparte, French statesman and military leader, former Emperor of France

A leader is a dealer in hope.

Never interrupt your enemy when he is making a mistake.

The reason most people fail instead of succeed is they trade what they want most for what they want at the moment.

Circumstances, what are circumstances? I make circumstances.

Courage isn't having the strength to go on - it is going on when you don't have strength.

Lawrence Bossidy, American author and retired businessman

Execution is the ability to mesh strategy with reality, align people with goals, and achieve the promised results.

Travis Bradberry, Author and consultant

One of the toughest things for leaders to master is kindness. Kindness shares credit and offers enthusiastic praise for others' work. It's a balancing act between being genuinely kind and not looking weak.

Remember, feedback is meant to address the problem, not the person.

Senator Bill Bradley, American politician, Basketball Hall of Famer, author

Leadership is unlocking people's potential to become better.

Ambition is the path to success. Persistence is the vehicle you arrive in.

Dorthea Brande, American writer and editor

Envisioning the end is enough to put the means in motion.

To guarantee success, act as if it were impossible to fail.

The Wright brothers flew through the smoke screen of impossibility.

A problem clearly stated is a problem half solved.

Sir Richard Branson, British business magnate, investor, author and philanthropist

Unless you dream, you're not going to achieve anything.

Brené Brown, Researcher, Storyteller, Texan

A leader is someone who holds her- or himself accountable for finding the potential in people and processes.

H. Jackson Brown, Jr., American author

The best preparation for tomorrow is doing your best today.

Les Brown, American motivational speaker, author, former radio DJ, and former television host
Don't let someone else's opinion become your reality.

You are never too old to set another goal or to dream a new dream.

I believe that life is a journey, often difficult and sometimes incredibly cruel, but we are well equipped for it if only we tap into our talents and gifts and allow them to blossom.

Too many of us are not living our dreams because we're living our fears.

Robert Browning, English poet and playwright
Ah, but a man's reach should exceed his grasp. Or what's a heaven for?

William Jennings Bryant, American orator and politician
Destiny is not a matter of chance; it is a matter of choice. It is not a thing to be wanted for, it is a thing to be achieved.

President James Buchanan, US President (1857-1861)
The task of leadership is not to put greatness into humanity, but to elicit it, for the greatness is already there.

Pearl Buck, American writer and novelist
   The secret of enjoying work is contained in one word - excellence. To know how to do something well is to enjoy it.

Milton Burle, American comedian and actor
   If opportunity doesn't knock, build a door.

Eric A. Burns, American author, playwright, media critic, and former broadcast journalist
   Greatness is more than potential. It is the execution of that potential. Beyond the raw talent. You need the appropriate training. You need the discipline. You need the inspiration. You need the drive.

Buddha, philosopher, mendicant, meditator, spiritual teacher, and religious leader who lived in ancient India
   The mind is everything.   What you think you become.

   Thousands of candles can be lighted from a single candle.   Happiness never decreases by being shared.

Carol Burnett, American actress, comedian, singer, and writer
   Only I can change my life. No one can do it for me.

   When you have a dream, you've got to grab it and never let go.

Leo Burnett, American advertising executive and the founder of Leo Burnett Company, Inc.

> When you reach for the stars you may not quite get one, but you won't come up with a handful of mud either.

William Bruce Cameron, American author, columnist, and humorist

> Not everything that can be counted counts, and not everything that counts can be counted.

Joseph Campbell, American professor of literature

> A hero is someone who has given his or her life to something bigger than oneself.

> People say that what we are seeking is a meaning for life. I don't think this is what we're really seeking. I think what we're seeking is an experience of being alive.

> We cannot cure the world of sorrows, but we can choose to live in joy.

> We must let go of the life we planned so as to accept the one that is waiting for us.

> Follow your bliss and the universe will open doors where there were only walls.

> A hero is someone who has given his or her life to something bigger than oneself.

> The cave you fear to enter holds the treasure you seek.

Follow your bliss and the universe will open doors where there were only walls.

Jack Canfield, American author, motivational speaker, corporate trainer, and entrepreneur
Don't worry about failures, worry about the chances you miss when you don't even try.

Richard Carlson, American author, psychotherapist, and motivational speaker
Choose being kind over being right and you'll be right every time.

Thomas Carlisle, a British historian, satirical writer, essayist, translator, philosopher, mathematician, and teacher
Go as far as you can see; when you get there, you'll be able to go further.

The lightning spark of thought generated in the solitary mind awakens its likeness in another mind.

Permanence, perseverance and persistence in spite of all obstacles, discouragements and impossibilities. It is this, that in all things distinguishes the strong souls from the weak.

Every noble work is at first impossible.

Show me the man you honor and I will know what kind of man you are.

Andrew Carnegie, Scottish-American industrialist, and philanthropist

No man will make a great leader who wants to do it all himself or get all the credit for doing it.

Dale Carnegie, American writer and lecturer, and the developer of courses in self-improvement, salesmanship, corporate training, public speaking, and interpersonal skills

Flaming enthusiasm, backed by horse sense and persistence, is the quality that most frequently makes for success.

You have it easily in your power to increase the sum total of this world's happiness now. How? By giving a few words of sincere appreciation to someone who is lonely or discouraged. Perhaps you will forget tomorrow the kind words you say today, but the recipient may cherish them over a lifetime.

President Jimmy Carter, US President (1977-1981)

If you fear making anyone mad, then you ultimately probe for the lowest common denominator of human achievement.

Rosalynn Carter, First Lady of the United States (1977-1981)

A leader takes people where they want to go. A great leader takes people where they don't necessarily want to go, but ought to be.

General George Casey, Four-star general who served
as the 36th Chief of Staff of the United States Army
Clarity and simplicity are the antidotes to complexity and uncertainty.

Carlos Castaneda, American author
The trick is in what one emphasizes. We either make ourselves miserable or we make ourselves strong. The amount of work is the same.

Marcus Porcius Cato, also known as Cato the Elder, the
Censor, the Wise, and the Ancient, was a Roman
soldier, senator and historian
After I'm dead, I'd rather have people ask why I have no monument than way I have one.

Francis Chan, American author on Christian subjects,
and a teacher and preacher
Our greatest fear should not be of failure, but of succeeding at things in life that don't really matter.

Chanakya, ancient Indian teacher, philosopher,
economist, jurist and royal advisor
Do not reveal what you have thought upon doing, but by wise council keep it secret being determined to carry it into execution.

Coco Chanel, French fashion designer and
businesswoman
The most courageous act is still to think for yourself. Aloud.

Dave Chappelle, American stand-up comedian, actor, writer, and producer
> The hardest thing to do is to be true to yourself, especially when everybody is watching.

Ralph Charell, Author
> Do your own thinking independently. Be the chess player, not the chess piece.

Brian Chesky, American billionaire technology entrepreneur
> Build something 100 people love, not something one million people kind of like.

Lord Chesterfield, British statesman, diplomat, and man of letters
> Know the true value of time; snatch, seize and enjoy every minute of it.

G. K. Chesterton, English writer, philosopher, lay theologian, and literary and art critic
> How you think when you lose determines how long it will be until you win.

> When it comes to life, the critical thing is whether you take things for granted or take them with gratitude.

Yvon Chouinard, American rock climber, environmentalist, and outdoor industry billionaire businessman

There's no difference between a pessimist who says, "Oh, it's hopeless, so don't bother doing anything," and an optimist who says, "Don't bother doing anything, it's going to turn out fine anyway." Either way, nothing happens.

Winston Churchill, British politician, army officer, and writer. Former Prime Minister of the United Kingdom (1940 - 1945), (1951-1955)

Success is walking from failure to failure with no loss of enthusiasm.

A pessimist sees the difficulty in every opportunity; an optimist sees the opportunity in every difficulty.

Some people dream of success while others wake up and work hard at it.

If you're going through hell, keep going.

Mountaintops inspire leaders but valleys mature them.

The price of greatness is responsibility.

We make a living by what we get, but we make a life by what we give.

Success is not final; failure is not fatal; it is the courage to continue that counts.

A man does what he must - in spite of personal consequences, in spite of obstacles and dangers and pressures — and that is the basis of all human morality.

Courage is what it takes to stand up and speak. Courage is also what it takes to sit down and listen.

Courage is the first of human qualities because it is the quality which guarantees all others.

Mountaintops inspire leaders but valleys mature them.

Timothy R. Clark, International consultant and trainer
Highly engaged employees make the customer experience. Disengaged employees break it.

Arthur C Clarke, British science fiction writer, science writer and futurist, inventor, undersea explorer, and television series host
The limits of the possible can only be defined by going beyond them into the impossible.

James Clear, author, entrepreneur, and photographer
We don't rise to the level of our goals; we fall to the level of our systems.

President Grover Cleveland, US President (1885-1889) (1893-1897)
Honor lies in honest toil.

President William J. Clinton, US President (1993-2001)
If you live long enough, you'll make mistakes. But if you learn from them, you'll be a better person. It's how you handle adversity, not how it affects you. The main thing is never quit, never quit, never quit.

George Clooney, American actor, director, producer and filmmaker
The only failure is not to try.

Paul Coelho, Brazilian lyricist and novelist
There is only one thing that makes a dream impossible to achieve: the fear of failure.

And when you want something, all the universe conspires in helping you achieve it.

Jim Collins, American researcher, author, speaker and consultant
Good is the enemy of great.

Alistair Cooke, British-born American writer, journalist, television personality and radio broadcaster
A professional is a person who can do his best at a time when he doesn't particularly feel like it.

President Calvin Coolidge, US President (1923-1929)
Those who trust to chance must abide by the results of chance.

Nothing in the world can take the place of Persistence. Talent will not; nothing is more common than unsuccessful men with talent. Genius will not; unrewarded genius is almost a proverb. Education will not; the world is full of educated derelicts. Persistence and Determination alone are omnipotent. The slogan "Press On" has solved and will always solve the problems of the human race.

No man ever listened himself out of a job.

All growth depends on activity. There is no development physically or intellectually without effort, and effort means work.

Bill Copeland, American poet, writer and historian
Try to be like a turtle - at ease in your own shell.

Barbara Corcoran, Real estate mogul and business expert
Leaders come in two flavors, expanders and containers. The best leadership teams have a mix of both.

The difference between successful people and others is how long they spend feeling sorry for themselves.

Norman Cousins, American political journalist, author, professor, and world peace advocate
Death is not the greatest loss in life. The greatest loss is what dies inside us while we live.

Stephen Covey, American educator, author, businessman and keynote speaker
> Effective leadership is putting first things first. Effective management is discipline, carrying it out.

> But until a person can say deeply and honestly, "I am what I am today because of the choices I made yesterday," that person cannot say, "I choose otherwise."

> What you do has far greater impact that what you say.
> Always treat your employees exactly as you want them to treat your best customers.

> Be patient with yourself. Self-growth is tender; its holy ground. There is no greater investment.

E. Joseph Cossman, Author, entrepreneur
> Obstacles are things a person sees when he takes his eyes off his goal.

Mark Cuban, American entrepreneur and investor
> Always look for the fool in the deal. If you don't find one, it's you.

Marie Curie, Polish and naturalized-French physicist and chemist who conducted pioneering research on radioactivity
> We must believe that we are gifted for something, and that this thing, at whatever cost, must be attained.

Roald Dahl, British novelist, short story writer, poet, screenwriter, and wartime fighter pilot

If you have good thoughts they will shine out of your face like sunbeams and you will always look lovely.

Sima Dahl, Branding expert, speaker, consultant

Celebrate the effort, for it is in the trying that you discover you.

Janet Dailey, American author

Someday is not a day of the week.

Charles Darwin, English naturalist, geologist and biologist

It is not the strongest of the species that survive, nor the most intelligent, but the one most responsive to change.

Leonardo Da Vinci, Italian polymath of the Renaissance whose areas of interest included invention, drawing, painting, sculpture, architecture, science, music, mathematics, engineering, literature, anatomy, geology, astronomy, botany, paleontology, and cartography

I have been impressed with the urgency of doing. Knowing is not enough; we must apply. Being willing is not enough; we must do.

It had long since come to my attention that people of accomplishment rarely sat back and let things happen to them. They went out and happened to things.

Who sows virtue reaps honor.

Learning never exhausts the mind.

Jimmy Dean, American country music singer, television host, actor, and businessman
I can't change the direction of the wind, but I can adjust my sails to always reach my destination.

Michael Dell, American billionaire businessman and philanthropist
As you start your journey, the first thing you should do is throw away that store-bought map and begin to draw your own.

Democritus, Ancient Greek pre-Socratic philosopher
More men have become great by practice than by nature.

Demosthenes, Greek statesman and orator of ancient Athens
Small opportunities are often the beginning of great enterprises.

Dame Judi Dench, English actress, artist and author
I think you should take your job seriously, but not yourself. That is the best combination.

Max De Pree, American businessman and writer
The first responsibility of a leader is to define reality. The last is to say thank you. In between, the leader is a servant.

Leadership is much more an art, a belief, a condition of the heart, than a set of things to do.

Leadership is liberating people to do what is required of them in the most effective and humane way possible.

Above all, leadership is a position of servanthood.

The leader is the servant who removes the obstacles that prevent people from doing their jobs.

Leaders don't inflict pain, they share pain.

Leadership is like third grade: it means repeating the significant things.

In the end, it is important to remember that we cannot become what we need to be by remaining what we are.

Antoine De Saint-Exupery, French writer, poet, aristocrat, journalist and pioneering aviator
Perfection is not when there is no more to add, but no more to take away.

Reneé Descartes, French philosopher, mathematician, and scientist
I think therefore I am.

Sheri Dew, American author and publisher
True leaders understand that leadership is not about them but about those they serve. It is not about exalting themselves but about lifting others up.

Matshona Dhliwayo, Canadian based Philosopher, Entrepreneur, and author
You either run with lions or walk with sheep.

Henri Martin Didon, French Dominican preacher, writer, educator, and promoter of youth sports
Citius, Altius, Fortius. The Olympic Motto

Annie Dillard, American author
A schedule defends from chaos and whim.

Peter Dinklage, American actor and producer
I hate that word: lucky. It cheapens a lot of hard work.

Diogenes of Sinope, Greek philosopher and one of the founders of Cynic philosophy
Wise leaders generally have wise counselors because it takes a wise person themselves to distinguish them.

Walt Disney, American entrepreneur, animator, writer, voice actor and film producer
The way to get started and to begin is doing.

If you can dream it, you can do it. And always remember that this whole thing was started by a mouse.

First, think. Second, dream. Third, believe. And finally, dare.

We keep moving forward, opening new doors, and doing new things, because we're curious and curiosity keeps leading us down new paths.

All our dreams can come true if we have the courage to pursue them.

Benjamin Disraeli, Former British Prime Minister (February – December 1868 and 1874-1880)
The greatest good you can do for another is not just to share your riches but to reveal to him his own.

I must follow the people. Am I not their leader?

Life is too short to be small.

Action may not always bring happiness, but there is not happiness without action.

Maxine Driscoll, Award winning educator
Great leaders harness personal courage, capture the hearts and minds of others and empower new leaders to make the world a better place.

Jack Dixon, Welsh rugby union player
> If you focus on results, you'll never change. If you focus on change, you'll get results.

Peter F. Drucker, Management consultant, educator and author
> Leadership is not magnetic personality, that can just as well be a glib tongue. It is not 'making friends and influencing people,' that is flattery. Leadership is lifting a person's vision to higher sights, the raising of a person's performance to a higher standard, the building of a personality beyond its normal limitations.

> Leadership is lifting a person's vision to high sights, the raising of a person's performance to a higher standard, the building of a personality beyond its normal limitations.

> The test of organization is not genius. It is its capacity to make common people achieve uncommon performance.

> Management is doing the right thing; leadership is doing the right things.

> It is the capacity to develop and improve their skills that distinguishes leaders from followers.

> Effective leadership is not about making speeches or being liked; leadership is defined by results, not attributes.

Your first and foremost job as a leader is to take charge of your own energy and then help to orchestrate the energy of those around you.

The effective executive does not make staffing decisions to minimize weaknesses but to maximize strength.

Time is the scarcest resource, and unless it is managed, nothing else can be managed.

What gets measured gets managed.

If you can't measure it, you can't improve it.

I have never encountered an executive who remains effective while tackling more than two tasks at a time.

Problem solving, however necessary, does not produce results. It prevents damage. Exploiting opportunities produces results.

People in any organization are always attached to the obsolete - the things that should have worked but did not, the things that once were productive and no longer are.

Whenever you see a successful business, someone once made a courageous decision.

People who don't take risks generally make about two big mistakes a year. People who do take risks generally make about two big mistakes a year.

It is the capacity to develop and improve their skills that distinguishes leaders from followers.

Charles Du Bos, French essayist and critic
The important thing is this: to be able to give up in any given moment all that we are for what we can become.

Tony Dungy, former professional American football player and coach in the National Football League
No excuses. No explanation. You don't win on emotion. You win on execution.

Bob Dylan, American singer-songwriter, author, and visual artist
A man is a success if he gets up in the morning and gets to bed at night, and in between he does what he wants to do.

People seldom do what they believe in. They do what is convenient, then repent.

Don't criticize what you can't understand.

Amelia Earhart, American aviation pioneer and author
Never interrupt someone doing something you said couldn't be done.

The most effective way to do it is to do it.

The most difficult thing is the decision to act, the rest is merely tenacity.

Worry retards reaction and makes clear-cut decisions impossible.

Courage is the price that life exacts for granting peace, the soul that knows it not, knows no release from little things.

A single act of kindness throws out roots in all directions, and the roots spring up and make new trees.

Wyatt Earp, Old West lawman and gambler in Cochise County, Arizona Territory, and a deputy marshal in Tombstone, AZ
Fast is fine, but accuracy is everything.

Thomas A. Edison, American inventor and businessman
Having a vision for what you want is not enough. Vision without execution is hallucination.

I have not failed. I've just found 10,000 ways that won't work.

If we did all the things we are capable of, we would literally astound ourselves.

Opportunity is missed by most people because it is dressed in overalls and looks like work.

Albert Einstein, German-born theoretical physicist

Everything should be made as simple as possible, but not simpler.

Reality is merely an illusion, albeit a very persistent one.

Strive not to be a success, but rather to be of value.

You have to learn the rules of the game. And then, you have to play it better than anyone else.

Reading, after a certain age, diverts the mind too much from its creative pursuits. Any man who reads too much and uses his own brain too little falls into lazy habits of thinking.

Logic will get you from A to B. Imagination will take you everywhere.

Out of clutter, find simplicity. From discord, find harmony. In the middle of difficulty lies opportunity.

A person who never made a mistake never tried anything new.

Great spirits have always found violent opposition from mediocrities. The latter cannot understand it when a man does not thoughtlessly submit to hereditary prejudices but honestly and courageously uses his intelligence.

President Dwight D. Eisenhower, US President (1953-1961)

You do not lead by hitting people over the head - that's assault, not leadership.

Pull the string, and it will follow wherever you wish. Push it, and it will go nowhere at all.

Always try to associate yourself with and learn as much as you can from those who know more than you do, who do better than you, who see more clearly than you.

Motivation is the art of getting people to do what you want them to do because they want to do it.

The supreme quality for leadership is unquestionably integrity. Without it, no real success is possible, no matter whether it is on a section gang, a football field, in an army, or in an office.

Leroy Eimes, Author

A leader is one who sees more than others see, who sees farther than others see, and who sees before others see.

Duke Ellington, American composer, pianist, and leader of a jazz orchestra

A problem is a chance for your to do your best.

Larry Ellison, American business magnate, investor, and philanthropist

> Both my mother and I were determined that we weren't going to stay on welfare. We always worked toward...having a better life. We never had any doubts that we would.

George Elliott, (Pen name for Mary Ann Evans) English novelist, poet, journalist, and translator

> It's never too late to be what you might have been.

T. S. Eliot, poet, essayist, publisher, playwright, literary critic and editor

> Only those who will risk going too far can possibly find out how far one can go.

Ralph Waldo Emerson, American essayist, lecturer, philosopher, and poet

> We aim above the mark to hit the mark.

> What lies behind us and what lies before us are tiny matters compared to what is within us.

> People only see what they are prepared to see.

> A man is what he thinks about all day long.

> The only person you are destined to become is the person you decide to be.

> Nothing great was ever achieved without enthusiasm.

Do not go where the path may lead, go instead where there is no path and leave a trail.

To be yourself in a world that is constantly trying to make you something else is the greatest accomplishment.

You cannot do a kindness too soon, for you never know how soon it will be too late.

Epictetus, Greek Stoic philosopher
It's not what happens to you, but how you react to it that matters.
Circumstances don't make the man; they only reveal him to himself.

Don't seek for everything to happen as you wish it would, but rather wish that everything happens as it actually will – then your life will flow well.

First say to yourself what you would be; and then do what you have to do.

Epicurus, Ancient Greek philosopher and sage
Do not spoil what you have by desiring what you have not; remember that what you. Now have was among the things. You only hoped for.

William Faulkner, American writer and Nobel Prize laureate
Always dream and shoot higher than you know you can do. Don't bother just to be better than your

contemporaries or predecessors. Try to be better than yourself.

Senator Dianne Feinstein, American politician, former US Senator
Ninety percent of leadership is the ability to communicate something people want.

Tim Ferriss, Tech investor/advisor, and author
Conditions are never perfect. 'Someday' is a disease that will take your dreams to the grave with you...If it's important to you and you want to do it 'eventually' just do it and correct course along the way.

Tina Fey, American actress, comedian, writer, producer, and playwright
In most cases being a good boss means hiring talented people and then getting out of their way.

Richard P. Feynman, American theoretical physicist, Nobel Prize for Physics
The first principle is that you must not fool yourself, and you are the easiest person to fool.

Debbi Fields, founder and spokesperson of Mrs. Fields Bakeries
The important thing is not being afraid to take a chance. Remember, the greatest failure is to not try. Once you find something you love to do, be the best at doing it.

Harvey S. Firestone, American businessman, and the founder of the Firestone Tire and Rubber Company

The growth and development of people is the highest calling of leadership

I believe fundamental honesty is the keystone of business.

Ella Fitzgerald, American jazz singer

It isn't where you came from. It's where you're going that counts.

Just don't give up trying to do what you really want to do. Where there is love and inspiration, I don't think you can go wrong.

Malcolm Forbes, American entrepreneur, publisher

If you have no critics, you'll likely have no success.

Henry Ford, American industrialist and business magnate

There is joy in work. There is no happiness except in the realization that we have accomplished something.

Wealth, like happiness, is never attained when sought after directly. It comes as a by-product of providing a useful service.

If everyone is moving forward together, then success takes care of itself. —

Before everything else, getting ready is the secret of success.

If there is any one secret of success, it lies in the ability to get the other person's point of view and see things from that person's angle as well as from your own.
There is no man living that cannot do more than he thinks he can.

I cannot discover that anyone knows enough to say definitely what is and what is not possible.

Whether you believe you can do a thing or not, you are right.

It has been my observation that most people get ahead during the time that others waste.

Whenever everything seems to be going against you, remember that the airplane takes off against the wind, not with it.

Failure is simply the opportunity to begin again, this time more intelligently.

There are no big problems, there are just a lot of little problems.
Quality means doing it right when no one is looking.

Don't find fault, find a remedy.

The man who will use his skill and constructive imagination to see how much he can give for a dollar, instead of how little he can give for a dollar, is bound to succeed.

Life is a series of experiences, each one of which makes us bigger, even though sometimes it is hard to realize this. For the world was built to develop character, and we must learn that the setbacks and grieves which we endure help us in our marching onward.

Coming together is a beginning; keeping together is progress; working together is success.

If everyone is moving forward together, then success takes care of itself.

Emmet Fox, Irish New Thought spiritual leader of the early 20th century
You must not under any pretense allow your mind to dwell on any thought that is not positive, constructive, optimistic, kind.

Anne Frank, German-born Dutch-Jewish diarist
How wonderful it is that nobody need wait a single moment before starting to improve the world.

Viktor E. Frankel, Austrian neurologist and psychiatrist and Holocaust survivor
What man actually needs is not a tensionless state but rather the striving and struggling for a worthwhile goal, a freely chosen task.

Benjamin Franklin, American polymath, one of the Founding Fathers of the United States, writer, printer, political philosopher, politician, Freemason, postmaster, scientist, inventor, humorist, civic activist, statesman, and diplomat
> Energy and persistence conquer all things.

> Diligence is the mother of good luck.

> Tell me and I forget. Teach me and I remember. Involve me and I learn.

> To succeed, jump as quickly at opportunities as you do at conclusions.

Sigmund Freud, Austrian neurologist and the founder of psychoanalysis
> One day, in retrospect, the years of struggle will strike you as the most beautiful.

Thomas Friedman, Political commentator and author
> Inspiring conduct has so much more of an impact than coercing it.

Robert Frost, American poet, Pulitzer Prize winner, Congressional Gold Medalist, poet laureate of Vermont
> The best way out is always through.

Two roads diverged in the wood, and I - I took the one less traveled by, and that has made all the difference.

Margaret Fuller, American journalist, editor, critic, and women's rights advocate
Today a reader, tomorrow a leader.

John Kenneth Galbraith, Canadian economist, public official and diplomat
All of the great leaders have had one characteristic in common: it was the willingness to confront unequivocally the major anxiety of their people in their time. This, and not much else, is the essence of leadership.

Mahatma Gandhi, Indian lawyer, anti-colonial nationalist, and political ethicist
I suppose leadership at one time meant muscles; but today it means getting along with people.

You must be the change you wish to see in the world.

The best way to find yourself is to lose yourself in the service of others. —

The future depends on what you do today.

Strength does not come from winning. Your struggles develop your strengths.

President James A. Garfield, US President (1881-1881)
Be fit for more than the thing you are now doing. Let everyone know that you have a reserve in yourself, — that you have more power than you are now using. If you are not too large for the place you occupy, you are too small for it.

Ideas control the world.

Judy Garland, American actress, singer, and dancer
Always be a first-rate version of yourself instead of a second-rate version of somebody else.

Bill Gates, American business magnate, software developer, investor, and philanthropist
Leaders need to provide strategy and direction and to give employees the tools that enable them to gather information and insight from around the world. Leaders shouldn't try to make every decision.

As we look ahead into the next century, leaders will be those who empower others.

The vision is really about empowering workers, giving them all the information about what's going on so they can do a lot more than they've done in the past.

Patience is a key element of success.

Success is a lousy teacher. It seduces smart people into thinking they can't lose.

The first rule of any technology used in a business is that automation applied to an efficient operation will magnify the efficiency. The second is that automation applied to an inefficient operation will magnify the inefficiency.

It's fine to celebrate success, but it is more important to heed the lessons of failure.

Your most unhappy customers are your greatest source of learning.

Harold Geneen, American Businessman
Leadership cannot really be taught. It can only be learned.

King George VI, King of the United Kingdom and the Dominions of the British Commonwealth (1936-1952)
The highest of distinctions is service to others.

Carlos Ghosn, Brazilian-born businessman
The role of leadership is to transform the complex situation into small pieces and prioritize them.

James Cardinal Gibbons, American prelate of the Catholic Church
There are no working hours for leaders.

Andre Gide, French author and winner of the Nobel Prize in Literature
Be faithful to that which exists within yourself.

Dan Gilbert, American businessman, investor, and philanthropist
Innovation is rewarded. Execution is worshipped.

Elizabeth Gilbert, American author
Stop wearing your wishbone where your backbone ought to be.

Henry Gilmer, American football player, member of the college football hall of fame
Look over your shoulder now and then to be sure someone's following you.

Jeffrey Gitomer, American author, professional speaker, and business trainer
There's no lotion or potion that will make sales faster and easier for you - unless your potion is hard work.
Your grammar is a reflection of your image. Good or bad, you have made an impression. And like all impressions, you are in total control.

Kick your own ass first.

Arnold Glasow, American businessman and author
One of the tests of leadership is the ability to recognize a problem before it becomes an emergency.

A good leader takes a little more than his share of the blame, a little less than his share of the credit.
— Arnold Glasow

Seth Godin, Author, former dot com business executive

> Leadership is the art of giving people a platform for spreading ideas that work.

> The secret of leadership is simple: Do what you believe in. Paint a picture of the future. Go there. People will follow.

> Leadership, on the other hand, is about creating change you believe in.

> How was your day? If your answer was "fine," then I don't think you were leading.

> In a battle between two ideas, the best one doesn't necessarily win. No, the idea that wins is the one with the most fearless heretic behind it.

> There's no shortage of remarkable ideas; what's missing is the will to execute them.

> Competent people are the most resistant to change.

> If it scares you, it might be a good thing to try.

Martha Graham, American modern dancer and choreographer

> There is a vitality, a life force, an energy that is translated through you; and because there is only one of you in all of time, this expression is unique.

Adam Grant, American psychologist and author
The most effective leaders aren't extraverts or introverts. They're ambiverts: people who strike a balance of talking and listening.

President Ulysses S. Grant, US President (1869-1877)
Two commanders on the same field are always one too many.

The most confident critics are generally those who know the least about the matter criticized.

Albert Gray, Canadian-born American businessman, politician and author
The common denominator of success is in forming the habit of doing things that failures don't like to do.

Farrah Gray, American businessman, investor, author, columnist, and motivational speaker
Build your own dreams, or someone else will hire you to build theirs.

Wayne Gretzky, Canadian former professional ice hockey player and former head coach
You miss 100% of the shots you don't take.

Chris Grosser, Photographer
Opportunities don't happen. You create them.

B. J. Gupta, Author
Hard work doesn't guarantee success, but it improves its chances.

Thich Nhat Hahn, Vietnamese Thiền Buddhist monk
and peace activist
> The miracle is not to walk on water. The miracle is to walk on the green earth, dwelling deeply in the present moment and feeling truly alive.

Robert Half, Founder, Robert Half International
> There is something more scarce, something rarer than ability. It is the ability to recognize ability.

Julian Hall, Entrepreneur, author
> Ideas are yesterday, execution is today and excellence will see you into tomorrow.

Herbie Hancock, Grammy Award-winning musician
> Forget about trying to compete with someone else. Create your own pathway. Create your own new vision.

John Hancock, American merchant, statesman, and
prominent Patriot of the American Revolution
> The greatest ability in business is to get along with others and influence their actions.

Grace Hansen, Author
> Don't be afraid your life will end; be afraid it will never begin.

Mark Victor Hansen, American inspirational and motivational speaker, trainer and author
Focused mind power is one of the strongest forces on earth.

Sydney J. Harris, American journalist, author
When I hear somebody sigh, 'Life is hard,' I am always tempted to ask, 'Compared to what?'

Henry Haskins, Stockbroker, author and man of letters
What lies behind us and what lies before us are tiny matters compared to what lies within us.

Ernest Hemingway, American journalist, novelist, short-story writer, and sportsman
When people talk, listen completely.

William Ernest Henley, English poet, critic and editor of the late Victorian era in England
I am the master of my fate; I am the captain of my soul.

Jim Henson, American puppeteer, animator, cartoonist, actor, inventor, filmmaker, and screenwriter
Life's like a movie; write your won ending, keep believing, keep pretending.

Audrey Hepburn, British actress and humanitarian
Nothing is impossible. The word itself says 'I'm possible!'

Heraclitus, Ancient Greek philosopher
No man ever steps in the same river twice, for it's not the same river and he's not the same man.

Herodotus, Ancient Greek historian
Haste in every business brings failures.

Great deeds are usually wrought at great risks.

Father Theodore M. Hesburgh, President of the University of Notre Dame
The very essence of leadership is that you have to have vision. You can't blow an uncertain trumpet.

Abraham Joshua Heschel, Polish-born American rabbi, Jewish theologian and Jewish philosopher
Wonder rather than doubt is the root of all knowledge.

Frances Hesselbein, former CEO of the Girl Scouts of the USA
Dispirited, unmotivated, unappreciated workers cannot compete in a highly competitive world.

Tommy Hilfiger, American fashion designer and founder of Tommy Hilfiger Corporation
The road to success is not easy to navigate, but with hard work, drive and passion, it's possible to achieve the American dream.

Napoleon Hill, American self-help author

Everyone enjoys doing the kind of work for which he is best suited.

Whatever the mind of man can conceive and believe, it can achieve.

Like the wind that carries one ship east and another west, the law of autosuggestion will lift you up or pull you down according to the way that you set your sails of thought.

Don't wait. The time will never be just right.

If you cannot do great things, do small things in a great way. —

Everyone enjoys doing the kind of work for which he is best suited.

The number one reason people fail in life is because they listen to their friends, family members and neighbors.

Dee Hock, Founder and former CEO of the Visa credit card association

Control is not leadership; management is not leadership; leadership is leadership. If you seek to lead, invest at least 50 percent of your time in leading yourself--your own purpose, ethics, principles, motivation, conduct. Invest at least 20 percent leading those with authority over you and 15 percent leading your peers.

Pete Hoekstra, Dutch-American politician, US Ambassador to the Netherlands, former member US house of representatives

Real leadership is leaders recognizing that they serve the people that they lead.

Ryan Holiday, American author, marketer, entrepreneur and founder of the creative advisory firm Brass Check

There is another apt Latin expression: Materiam superabat opus. (The workmanship is better than the material.) The material we've been given genetically, emotionally, financially, that's where we begin. We don't control that. We do control what we make of that material, and whether we squander it.

Oliver Wendell Holmes, American jurist who served as an Associate Justice of the Supreme Court of the United States

The great thing in this world is not so much where you stand, as in what direction you're moving.

John Holt, American author and educator

The true test of character is to how much we know how to do, but how we behave when we don't know what to do.

Lou Holtz, Former American football player, coach, analyst, speaker and author

Don't ever promise more than you can deliver, but always deliver more than you promise.

Winners and losers aren't born, they are the products of how they think.

The man who complains about the way the ball bounces is likely the one who dropped it.

Ability is what you're capable of doing. Motivation determines what you do. Attitude determines how well you do it.

I can't believe that God put us on this earth to be ordinary.

Nothing is as good as it seems, and nothing is as bad as it seems. Somewhere in between lies realty.

When all is said and done, more is said than done.

You're never as good as everyone tells you when you win, and you're never as bad as they say when you lose.

Winners embrace hard work. They love the discipline of it, the tradeoff they're making to win. Losers, on the other hand, see it as punishment. And that's the difference.

It's not the load that breaks you down, it's the way you carry it.

President Herbert Hoover, US President (1929-1933)
Words without actions are the assassins of idealism.

Rear Admiral Grace Hopper, American computer scientist and United States Navy rear admiral
You manage things; you lead people.

Horace, Roman lyric poet during the time of Augustus
Don't think, just do.

Kin Hubbard, nationally-known American cartoonist, humorist, and journalist
Being an optimist after you've got the very thing you want doesn't count.

Arianna Huffington, Greek-American author, syndicated columnist, and businesswoman
Fearlessness is like a muscle. I know from my own life that the more I exercise it, the more natural it becomes not to let my fears run me.

James Humes, Author and former presidential speechwriter
The art of communication is the language of leadership.
Every time you have to speak, you are auditioning for leadership.

Ian Hutchinson, English professional motorcycle road racer
Your number one customers are your people. Look after employees first and then customers last.

Thomas Huxley, English biologist and anthropologist specializing in comparative anatomy
The rung of a ladder was never meant to rest upon, but only to hold a man's foot long enough to enable him to put the other somewhat higher.

Michael Hyatt, American author, podcaster, blogger, speaker, and the former chairman and CEO of Thomas Nelson
Vision attracts resources.

Jeffrey Immelt, American business executive
Surviving a failure gives you more self-confidence. Failures are a great learning tools...but they must be kept to a minimum.

Washington Irving, American short-story writer, essayist, biographer, historian, and diplomat of the early 19th century
Little minds are tamed and subdued by misfortune, but great minds rise above them.

President Andrew Jackson, US President (1829-1837)
Any man worth his salt will stick up for what he believes right, but it takes a slightly better man to acknowledge instantly and without reservation that he is in error.

Any man worth his salt will stick up for what he believes right, but it takes a slightly better man to acknowledge instantly and without reservation that he is in error.

Phil Jackson, American former professional basketball player, coach, and executive in the National Basketball Association

The strength of the team is each member. The strength of each member is the team.

Josh James, American professional baseball player

When you find an idea that you just can't stop thinking about, that's probably a good one to pursue.

William James, American philosopher and psychologist, and the first educator to offer a psychology course in the United States

We need only in cold blood act as if the thing in question were real and it will. Become infallibly real. By growing into such a connection with our life that it will become real. It will become so knit with habit and emotion that our interests in it will be those which characterize belief.

If you only care enough for a result, you almost certainly attain it. If you wish to be rich you will be rich, if you wish to be learned you will be learned. If you wish to be good you will be good. Only you must then really wish these things and wish them exclusively and not wish at the same time hundred other incompatible things just as strongly.

Act if what you do makes a difference. It does.

It is our attitude at the beginning of a difficult task which, more than anything else, will affect its successful outcome.

The greatest discovery of my generation is that human beings can alter their lives by altering their attitudes of mind.

Be not afraid of life. Believe that it is worth living, and your belief will help create the fact.

Jay-Z, American rapper, songwriter, record producer, record executive, and businessman
I love what I do, and when you love what you do, you want to be the best at it.

President Thomas Jefferson, US President (1801-1809)
Nothing can stop the man with the right mental attitude from achieving his goal; nothing on earth can help the man with the wrong mental attitude.

Nothing gives a person so much advantage over another as to remain always cool and unruffled under all circumstances.

Do you want to know who you are? Don't ask. Act! Action will delineate and define you.

Determine never to be idle. No person will have occasion to complain of the want of time who never loses any. It is wonderful how much may be done if we are always doing.

I find the harder I work the more luck I seem to have.

Whenever you do a thing, act as if all the world were watching.

In matters of style, swim with the current. In matters of principle, stand like a rock.

We have but two ears and one mouth, so that we may listen twice as much as we speak.

The wise know their weakness too well to assume infallibility; and he who knows most, knows best how little he knows.

Mae Jemison, American engineer, physician, and former NASA astronaut
Never limit yourself because of others' limited imagination; never limit others because of your own limited imagination.

St. Jerome, Latin priest, confessor, theologian, and historian
Good, better, best. Never let it rest 'til your good is better and your better is best.

Steve Jobs, American business magnate, industrial designer, investor, and media proprietor
My job is not to be easy on people. My job is to take these great people we have and to push them and make them even better.

Be a yardstick of quality. Some people aren't used to an environment where excellence is expected.

To me, ideas are worth nothing unless executed. They are just a multiplier. Execution is worth millions.
You have to be burning with an idea, or a problem, or a wrong that you want to right. If you're not passionate enough from the start, you'll never stick it out.

Innovation distinguishes between a leader and a follower.
Have the courage to follow your heart and intuition. They somehow know what you truly want to become.

Dean Johnson, Musician and party promoter
Listening is an art that requires attention over talent, spirit over ego, others over self.

Dwayne Johnson, American-Canadian actor, producer, businessman, and former professional wrestler and football player
All success begins with self-discipline. It starts with you.

Be humble. Be hungry. And be the hardest worker in the room.

President Lyndon B. Johnson, US President (1963-1969)

Yesterday is not ours to recover, but tomorrow is ours to win or to lose.

Doing what is right isn't the problem. It is knowing what is right. — Lyndon B. Johnson
You aren't learning anything when you're talking.

There are no problems we cannot solve together, and very few that we can solve by ourselves.

Samuel Johnson, English writer, poet, playwright, essayist, moralist, literary critic, biographer, editor, and lexicographer

Great works are performed not by strength but by perseverance.

Spencer Johnson, American physician and author

What would you do if you weren't afraid?

Art Jonak, Entrepreneur and Network Marketer

Those who spend their time looking for the faults in others usually make no time to correct their own.

David Star Jordan, American ichthyologist, educator, eugenicist, and peace activist

Wisdom is knowing what to do next, skill is knowing how to do it, and virtue is doing it.

Michael Jordan, Former NBA player and principal owner of the Charlotte Hornets of the National Basketball Association

Earn your leadership every day.

Some people want it to happen, some wish it would happen, others make it happen.

I've failed over and over again in my life. And that is why I succeed.

I can accept failure; everyone fails at something. But I can't accept not trying.

Obstacles don't have to stop you. If you run into a wall, dot turn around and give up. Figure out how to climb it, go through it, or work around it.

If you accept the expectations of others, especially negative ones, then you never will change the outcome.

Talent wins games, but teamwork and intelligence wins championships.

Robert Jordan, American author of epic fantasy

There is one rule above all others, for being a man. Whatever comes, face it on your feet.

Erica Jong, American novelist, satirist, and poet

You take your life in your own hands, and what happens? A terrible thing: no one to blame.

Henry J. Kaiser, American industrialist known as the father of modern American shipbuilding
> Live daringly, boldly, fearlessly. Taste the relish to be found in competition - inhaling put forth the best within you.

> When your work speaks for itself, don't interrupt.

Rob Kalin, Entrepreneur
> The last 10% it takes to launch something takes as much energy as the first 90%.

Mindy Kaling, American comedian, actress, and writer
> Sometimes you just have to put on lip gloss and pretend to be psyched.

Ingvar Kamprad, Swedish business magnate, founder of IKEA
> Only those who are asleep make no mistakes.

Alphose Karr, French critic, journalist, and novelist
> Some people are always grumbling because roses have thorns; I am thankful that thorns have roses.

Helen Keller, American author, political activist, and lecturer
> Optimism is the faith that leads to achievement.

> Security is mostly a superstition. Life is either a daring adventure, or nothing.

> Keep your face to the sunshine and you cannot see a shadow.

Never bend your head. Always hold it high. Look the world straight in the eye.

Alone we can do so little; together we can do so much.

President John F. Kennedy, US President (1961-1963)
Once you say you're going to settle for second, that's what happens to you in life.

Victory has a hundred fathers and defeat is an orphan.

The time to repair the roof is when the sun is shining.

As we express our gratitude, we must never forget that the highest appreciation is not to utter words, but to live by them.

Conformity is the jailer of freedom and the enemy of growth.

Change is the law of life. And those who look only to the past or present are certain to miss the future.

There are risks and costs to action. But they are far less than the long range risks of comfortable inaction.

Leadership and learning are indispensable to each other.

Charles Kettering, American inventor, engineer, and businessman

It doesn't matter if you try and try and try again and fail. It does matter if you try and fail and fail to try again.

There exist limitless opportunities in every industry. Where there is an open mind, there will always be a frontier.

Believe and act as if it were impossible to fail.

John Maynard Keynes, 1st Baron Keynes, British economist

Ideas shape the course of history.

Victor Kiam, American entrepreneur

Even if you fall on your face, you're still moving forward.

Dr. Martin Luther King Jr., American Christian minister and activist who became the most visible spokesperson and leader in the Civil Rights Movement

A genuine leader is not a searcher for consensus, but a molder of consensus.

We are not makers of history; we are made by history.

If you can't fly, then run; if you can't run, then walk; if you can't walk, then crawl; but whatever you do, you have to keep moving forward.

Life's most persistent and urgent question is, 'What are you doing for others?'

Not everybody can be famous. But everybody can be great, because greatness is determined by service.

You are not only responsible for what you say, but also for what you do not say.

The time is always right to do the right thing.

The ultimate measure of a man is not where he stands in moments of comfort and convenience, but where he stands at times of challenge and uncertainty.

The time is always right to do the right thing.

Forgiveness is not an occasional act; it is a permanent attitude.

Even if I knew that tomorrow the world would go to pieces, I would still plant my apple tree.

Stephen King, American author of horror, supernatural fiction, suspense, and fantasy novels
Get busy living or get busy dying.

individual from the successful one is a lot of hard work.

The scariest moment is always just before you start.

If you can you should, and if you're brave enough to start, you will.

Robert Kiyosaki, American businessman and author
In the real world, the smartest people are people who make mistakes and learn. In school, the smartest people don't make mistakes.

Henry Kissinger, American politician, diplomat, and geopolitical consultant
The task of the leader is to get their people from where they are to where they have not been.

Phillip Knight, American business magnate and philanthropist
The trouble in America is not that we are making too many mistakes, but that we are making too few.

Ray Kroc, American fast-food tycoon
The quality of a leader is reflected in the standards they set for themselves.

Luck is a dividend of sweat. The more you sweat, the luckier you get.

Mike Krzyzewski, American college basketball coach, former coach of US Olympic team
Leadership is an ever-evolving position.

Aung San Suu Kyi, Burmese politician, diplomat, author, and a 1991 Nobel Peace Prize laureate
The only real prison is fear and the only real freedom is freedom from fear.

Louis L'Amour, American novelist and short-story writer
> There will come a time when you believe everything is finished. That will be the beginning.

Jean de La Fontaine, French fabulist and one of the most widely read French poets of the 17th century
> Man is so made that when anything fires his soul, impossibilities vanish.

Dalai Lama, Dalai Lamas are important monks of the Gelug school, the newest school of Tibetan Buddhism
> Happiness is not something ready-made. It comes from your own actions.

> Remember that not getting what you want is sometimes a wonderful stroke of luck.

> Be kind whenever possible. It is always possible.

> When you talk, you are only repeating what you already know. But if you listen, you may learn something new.

Karen Lamb, Author
> A year from now you will wish you had started today.

Ann Landers, Former syndicated advice columnist
> Opportunities are usually disguised as hard work, so most people don't recognize them.

Doug Larson, Columnist and editor
Some of the world's greatest feats were accomplished by people not smart enough to know they were impossible.

Estee Lauder, American businesswoman
I've never dreamt of success. I worked for it.

Ralph Lauren, American fashion designer,
philanthropist, and billionaire businessman
A leader has the vision and conviction that a dream can be achieved. He inspires the power and energy to get it done.

Bruce Lee, Hong Kong American actor, director,
martial artist, martial arts instructor, and philosopher
The successful warrior is the average man with laser like focus.

A goal is not always meant to be reached; it often serves simply as something to aim at.

The consciousness of self is the greatest hindrance to the proper execution of all physical action.

One does not accumulate but eliminate. It is not daily increase but daily decrease. The height of cultivation always runs to simplicity.

Robert E. Lee, American and Confederate soldier
I cannot trust a man to control others who cannot control himself.

Maxime Lagacé, Canadian professional ice hockey goaltender

> Make people feel like the hero of their journey and they will do more.

Patrick Lencioni, American author

> Great teams do not hold back with one another. They are unafraid to air their dirty laundry. They admit their mistakes, their weaknesses, and their concerns without fear of reprisal.

John Lennon, English singer, songwriter and peace activist

> Life is what happens while you're busy making other plans.

C. S. Lewis, British writer and lay theologian

> You are never too old to set another goal or to dream a new dream.

> Hardships often prepare ordinary people for an extraordinary destiny.

> You can't go back and change the beginning, but you can start where you are and change the ending.

> We meet no ordinary people in our lives.

President Abraham Lincoln, US President (1861-1865)

> Whatever you are, be a good one.

> Don't worry when you are not recognized but strive to be worthy of recognition.

Always bear in mind that your own resolution to succeed is more important than any one thing.

I walk slowly, but never backward.

Be with a leader when he is right, stay with him when he is still right, but, leave him when he is wrong.

You can tell the greatness of a man by what makes him angry.

Nearly all men can stand adversity, but if you want to test a man's character, give him power.

Character is like a tree and reputation like a shadow. The shadow is what we think of it; the tree is the real thing.

You can fool all the people some of the time, and some of the people all the time, but you cannot fool all the people all the time.

How many legs does a dog have if you call his tail a leg? Four. Saying that a tail is a leg doesn't make it a leg.

Tact is the ability to describe others as they see themselves.

Do I not destroy my enemies when I make them my friends?

Books serve to show a man that those original thoughts of his aren't very new at all.

Dr. Henry Link, Psychologist and author
We generate fears while we sit. We overcome them by action. Fear is nature's way of warning us to get busy.

John Locke, English philosopher and physician
Education begins the gentleman, but reading, good company and reflection must finish him.

Vince Lombardi, American football coach, and executive in the National Football League
Leaders aren't born, they are made. And they are made just like anything else, through hard work. And that's the price we'll have to pay to achieve that goal, or any goal

Perfection is not attainable, but if we chase perfection we can catch excellence.

The difference between a successful person and others is not a lack of strength, not a lack of knowledge, but rather a lack of will.

Jennifer Lopez, American actress, singer, dancer, fashion designer, producer, and businesswoman
You get what you give.

Demi Lovato, American singer, songwriter, actress, and television personality
> No matter what you're going through, there's a light at the end of the tunnel.

Max Lucado, Christian author and pastor at Oak Hills Church in San Antonio, Texas
> A man who wants to lead the orchestra must turn his back on the crowd.

H.E. Luccock, American Methodist minister and professor of Homiletics at Yale Divinity School
> No one can whistle a symphony. It takes a while whole orchestra to play it.

Lucretius, Roman poet and philosopher
> Constant dripping hollows out a stone.

Robert J. Lumsden, Best-selling author
> A good criterion for measuring success in life is the number of people you have made happy.

Jack Ma, Chinese business magnate, investor and politician
> A leader should have higher grit and tenacity and be able to endure what the employees can't.

Ian MacLaren, Minister and author
> Be kind for everyone you meet is fighting a hard battle.

General Douglas MacArthur, American five-star
general and Field Marshal of the Philippine Army.

There is no security on the Earth, there is only opportunity.

Never give an order that can't be obeyed.

A true leader has the confidence to stand alone, the courage to make tough decisions, and the compassion to listen to the needs of others. He does not set out to be a leader but becomes one by the equality of his actions and the integrity of his intent. — General Douglas MacArthur

Niccolò Machiavelli, Italian renaissance diplomat,
philosopher and writer

He who wishes to be obeyed must know how to command.

It is not titles that honour men, but men that honour titles.

Whoever desires constant success must change his conduct with the times.

I'm not interested in preserving the status quo; I want to overthrow it.

Where the willingness is great, the difficulties cannot be great.

The first method for estimating the intelligence of a ruler is to look at the men around him.

It must be remembered that there is nothing more difficult to plan, more doubtful of success, nor more dangerous to manage than a new system. For the initiator has the enmity of all who would profit by the preservation of the old institution and merely lukewarm defenders in those who gain by the new ones.

Everyone sees what you appear to be, few experience what you really are.

There is no other way to guard yourself against flattery than by making men understand that telling you the truth will not offend you.

Men are driven by two principal impulses, either by love or by fear.

Never was anything great achieved without danger.

All courses of action are risky, so prudence is not in avoiding danger (it's impossible), but in calculating risk and acting decisively. Make mistakes of ambition and not mistakes of sloth. Develop the strength to do bold things, not the strength to suffer.

A man who is used to acting in one way never changes; he must come to ruin when the times, in changing are no longer in harmony with his ways.

A prudent man should always follow in the path trodden by great men and imitate those who are most excellent, so that if he does not attain to their greatness, at any rate he will get some tinge of it.

President James Madison, US President (1809-1817)
Knowledge will forever govern ignorance, and a people who mean to be their own governors, must arm themselves with the power knowledge gives.

Nelson Mandela, Former President of South Africa (1994-1999), anti-apartheid revolutionary, political leader and philanthropist
It is better to lead from behind and to put others in front, especially when you celebrate victory when nice things occur. You take the front line when there is danger. Then people will appreciate your leadership.

There is no passion to be found in settling for a life that is less than the one you are capable of living.

It always seems impossible until it's done.

A winner is a dreamer who never gives up.

I learned that courage was not the absence of fear, but the triumph over it. The brave man is not he who does not feel afraid, but he who conquers that fear.

Og Mandingo, American author
> Beginning today, treat everyone you meet as if they were going to be dead by midnight. Extend to them all the care, kindness and understanding you can muster, and do it with no thought of any reward. Your life will never be the same again.

Robert F. Mager, American psychologist and author
> If you're not sure where you are going, you're liable to end up someplace else.

Steve Maraboli, Speaker, bestselling Author, and Behavioral Science Academic
> Happiness is not the absence of problems; it's the ability to deal with them.

Orison Swett Marden, American inspirational author
> There is no investment you can make which will pay you so well as the effort to scatter sunshine and good cheer through your establishment.

Bruno Mars, American singer, songwriter, record producer, multi-instrumentalist, and dancer
> You can't knock on opportunity's door and not be ready.

Ralph Marston, Author, the Daily Motivator
> Excellence is not a skill it's an attitude.

Steve Martin, American actor, comedian, writer, and musician
> Be so good they can't ignore you.

John C. Maxwell, American author, speaker and pastor
A good leader is a person who takes a little more than his share of the blame and a little less than his share of the credit.

If you want to lead on the highest level, be willing to serve on the lowest.

Successful and unsuccessful people do not vary greatly in their abilities. They vary in their desire to reach their potential.

Tend to the people, and they will tend to the business.

The higher you want to climb, the more you need leadership. The greater the impact you want to make, the greater your influence needs to be.

Tend to the people, and they will tend to the business.

Teamwork makes the dream work.

Benjamin Mays, American Baptist minister and civil rights leader
The tragedy in life doesn't lie in not reaching your goal. The tragedy lies in having no goal to reach.

Harold R. McAlindon, Peruvian-born American Author, Writer, Management Speaker and Businessman
Do not follow where the path may lead. Go instead where there is no path and leave a trail.

Helen McCabe, Former editor-in-chief, Australian Women's Weekly
> One bad day from one member of my staff doesn't mean they are not really good at their jobs the rest of the time. I play a long game in terms of management.

Reba McEntire, American country singer, songwriter, actress, and record producer
> To succeed in life, you need three things: a wishbone, a backbone, and a funny bone.

Donald McGannon, Broadcasting executive
> Leadership is an action, not a position

Bryant H. McGill, author, activist, and social entrepreneur
> One of the most sincere forms of respect is actually listening to what another has to say.

President William McKinley, US President (1897-1901)
> Half-heartedness never won a battle.

Admiral William McRaven, Retired United States Navy four-star admiral, educator, and author
> Following is one of the most underrated aspects of leadership. I have seen many a good [military unit] underachieve because someone...thought the commander was incompetent, and quietly worked to undermine his authority.

Peter McWilliams, American self-help author
> Be willing to be uncomfortable. Be comfortable being uncomfortable. It may get tough, but it's a small price to pay for living a dream.

Margaret Mead, American cultural anthropologist, author and speaker
> Never doubt that a small group of thoughtful committed citizens can change the world. Indeed, it is the only thing that ever has.

Brad Meltzer, American political thriller novelist, non-fiction writer, TV show creator, and comic book author
> We are all ordinary. We are all boring. We are all spectacular. We are all shy. We are all bold. We are all heroes. We are all helpless. It just depends on the day.

Herman Melville, American novelist, short story writer and poet
> It is better to fail in originality than to succeed in imitation.

> Truth uncompromisingly told will always have its jagged edges.

Thomas Merton, American Trappist monk, writer, theologian, mystic, poet, social activist, and religious scholar
> The biggest temptation is to settle for too little.

Paul J. Meyer, Self-improvement industry pioneer
The only honest measure of your success is what you are doing compared with your true potential.

Jillian Michaels, American personal trainer, businesswoman, author and television personality
It's not about perfect. It's about effort. And when you bring that effort every single day, that's where transformation happens.

Michelangelo, Italian sculptor, painter, architect and poet of the High Renaissance
The greatest danger for most of us is not that our aim is too high and we miss it, but that it's too low and we reach it.

Lord, grant that I may always desire more than I can accomplish.

I am still learning.

John Steward Mill, British philosopher, political economist, and civil servant
One person with a belief is equal to 99 who have only interests.

Ralph Moody, American author
Always remember, Son, the best boss is the one who bosses the least. Whether it's cattle, or horses, or men; the least government is the best government.

Mary Tyler Moore, American stage, film, and television
actress, producer and social advocate
> Take chances, make mistakes. That's how you
> grow. Pain nourishes your courage. You have to
> fail in order to practice being brave.

Mother Teresa, Albanian-Indian Roman Catholic nun
and missionary
> I alone cannot change the world, but I can cast a
> stone across the water to create many ripples.

> Kind words are short and easy to speak, but their
> echoes are truly endless.

Charlie Munger, American investor, businessman,
former real estate attorney, and philanthropist
> You're not going to get very far in life based on what
> you already know. You're going to advance in life
> by what you're going to learn after you leave here.

Elon Musk, engineer, industrial designer,
philanthropist, and technology entrepreneur
> If something is important enough, even if the odds
> are against you, you should still do it.

> There is a tremendous bias against taking risks.
> Everyone is trying to optimize their ass-covering.

Ralph Nader, American political activist, author,
lecturer, and attorney
> The function of leaders is to produce more leaders,
> not more followers.

Akkineni Nagarjuna, Indian film actor, producer, television presenter, and entrepreneur

Although you may spend your life killing, you will not exhaust all your foes. But if you quell your own anger your real enemy will be slain.

Joe Namath, American former professional football player, Pro Football Hall of Fame inductee

If you aren't going all the way, why go at all?

John Neal, Author and art/literary critic

Hardship is the native soil of manhood and self-reliance.

Willie Nelson, American musician, actor, and activist

Once you replace negative thoughts with positive ones, you'll start having positive results.

Patrick Ness, British-American author, journalist, lecturer and screenwriter

To say you have no choice is to relieve yourself of responsibility.

Paul Newman, American actor, film director, producer, race car driver, IndyCar owner, entrepreneur, and philanthropist

When you see the right thing to do, you'd better do it.

Friedrich Nietzsche, German philosopher, cultural critic, composer, poet, philologist, and scholar of Latin and Greek

> To do great things is difficult; but to command great things is more difficult.

> That which does not kill us makes us stronger.

Earl Nightingale, American radio speaker and author

> Whatever we plant in our subconscious mind and nourish with repetition and emotion will one day become a reality.

> Success is the progressive realization of a worthy ideal.

> Our attitude towards life determines life's attitude toward us.

> We become what we think about.

> All you need is the plan, the road map and the courage to press on to your destination.

Florence Nightingale, British social reformer, statistician, and founder of modern nursing

> I attribute my success to this: I never gave or took any excuse.

Hussein Nishah, 16th-century Punjabi Sufi poet

> Treat people the way you want to be treated. Talk to people the way you want to be talked to. Respect is earned not given.

Charles Nix, American designer, typographer, and educator
Looking good isn't self-importance; it's self-respect.

President Richard M. Nixon, US President (1969-1974)
The man of thought who will not act is ineffective; the man of action who will not think is dangerous.

Defeat doesn't finish a man, quit does. A man is not finished when he's defeated. He's finished when he quits.

The finest steel has to go through the hottest fire.

Chuck Norris, American martial artist, actor, film producer and screenwriter
A lot of times, people look at the negative side of what they feel they can't do. I always look on the positive side of what I can do.

President Barack H. Obama, US President (2009-2017)
We need to internalize this idea of excellence. Not many folks spend a lot of time trying to be excellent.

Change will not come if we wait for some other person or some other time. We are the one's we've been waiting for. We are the change we seek.

You can't let your failures define you. You have to let your failures teach you.

Progress will come in fits and starts. It's not always a straight line. It's not always smooth path.

If you're walking down the right path and you're willing to keep walking, eventually you'll make progress.

Change will not come if we wait for some other person or some other time. We are the one's we've been waiting for. We are the change we seek.

Conan O'Brien, American television host, comedian, writer, podcaster, and producer
If you work really hard and you're kind, amazing things will happen.

William of Occam, English Franciscan friar, scholastic philosopher, and theologian
It is vain to do with more what can be done with less.

Frank Ocean, American singer, songwriter, record producer, and photographer
Work hard in silence, let success be your noise.

Bill Owens, American photographer, photojournalist, brewer and editor
True leadership lies in guiding others to success--in ensuring that everyone is performing at their best, doing the work they are pledged to do and doing it well.

Jesse Owens, American track and field athlete and four-time gold medalist

> We all have dreams. But in order to make dreams come into reality, it takes an awful lot of determination, dedication, self-discipline and effort.

Al Pacino, American actor and filmmaker

> Character is how you treat those who can do nothing for you.

> You are only as good as the chances you take.

Larry Page, American computer scientist and internet entrepreneur

> My jobs as a leader is to make sure everybody in the company has great opportunities, and that they feel they're having a meaningful impact.

Satchel Paige, American Negro league baseball and Major League Baseball pitcher

> iWork like you don't need the money. Love like you've never been hurt. Dance like nobody's watching.

Arnold Palmer, American professional golfer and businessman

> Always make a total effort, even when the odds are against you.

Jamie Paolinetti, Writer/director

> Limitations live only in our minds. But if we use our imaginations, our possibilities become limitless.

Rosa Parks, American civil rights activist
Each person must live their life as a model for others.

I have learned over the years that when one's mind is made up, this diminishes fear; knowing what must be done does away with fear.

Dolly Parton, American singer, songwriter, multi-instrumentalist, record producer, actress, author, businesswoman, and humanitarian
If your actions create a legacy that inspires others to dream more, learn more, do more and become more, then, you are an excellent leader.

If you don't like the road you're walking on, start paving another one.

Louis Pasteur, French biologist, microbiologist and chemist
Chance favors the prepared mind.

Let me tell you the secret that has led me to my goals: my strength lies solely in my tenacity.

Patanjali, sage in India, thought to be the author of a number of Sanskrit works
When you are inspired by some great purpose, some extraordinary project, all your thoughts break their bonds.

General George S. Patton, A general of the US Army
Be willing to make decisions. That's the most important quality in a good leader

If you are going to win any battle, you have to do one thing: You have to make the mind run the body. Never let the body tell the mind what to do. The body is never tired if the mind is not tired.

Never tell people how to do things. Tell them what to do and they will surprise you with their ingenuity.

Norman Vincent Peale, American minister and author
Empty pockets never held anyone back. Only empty heads and empty hearts can do that.

Change your thoughts and change your world.

This is one of the greatest laws in the universe. Fervently do I wish I had discovered it as a very young man. It dawned upon me much later in life and I've found it to be one of the greatest, if not my greatest discovery outside of my relationship with God. And the great law briefly and simply stated is that if you think in negative terms you'll get negative results. If you think in positive terms, you will achieve positive results. That is the simple fact which is at the basis of an astonishing law of prosperity and success in three words "believe and succeed."

M. Scott Peck, American psychiatrist and best-selling author

>Servant-leadership is more than a concept, it is a fact. Any great leader, by which I also mean an ethical leader of any group, will see herself or himself as a servant of that group and will act accordingly.

William Penn, writer, early member of the Religious Society of Friends, and founder of the English North American colony the Province of Pennsylvania

>Time is what we want most, but what we use worst.

James Cash Penny, American businessman and entrepreneur who founded the J. C. Penney stores

>Give me a stock clerk with a goal, and I will give you a man who will make history. Give me a man without a goal and I will give you a stock clerk.

H. Ross Perot, American business magnate, billionaire, philanthropist, and politician

>Most people give up just when they are about to achieve success. They quit on the one-yard line. They give up at the last minute of the game, one foot from a winning touchdown.

>Inventories can be managed, but people must be led.

General John J. Pershing, General of the US Armies

>A competent leader can get efficient service from poor troops, while on the contrary, an incapable leader can demoralize the best of troops.

Laurence J. Peter, Canadian educator and "hierarchiologist" best known to the general public for the formulation of the Peter principle

There are two kinds of failures: those who thought and never did, and those who did and never thought.

Tom Peters, American writer, business consultant

The thing that keeps a business ahead of the competition is excellence in execution.

Pablo Picasso, Spanish painter, sculptor, printmaker, ceramicist, stage designer, poet and playwright

Action is the foundational key to all success.

Only put off until tomorrow what you are willing to die having left undone.

President Franklin Pierce, US President (1853-1857)

If your past is limited, your future is boundless.

Remember that time is money.

Plato, Athenian philosopher during the Classical period in Ancient Greece, founder of the Platonist school of thought, and the Academy, the first institution of higher learning in the Western world

Human behavior flows from three main sources: desire, emotion, and knowledge.

Reality is created in the mind; we can change our reality by changing our mind. — Plato

The beginning is the most important part of the work.

Those who intend on becoming great should love neither themselves or their own things, but only what is just, whether it happens to be done by themselves or others.

Courage is knowing what not to fear.

We can easily forgive a child who is afraid of the dark; the real tragedy of life is when men are afraid of the light.

People are like dirt. They can either nourish you and help you grow as a person or they can stunt your growth and make you wilt and die.

Plotinus, Hellenistic philosopher who lived in Roman Egypt

Knowledge, if it does not determine action, is dead to us.

Plutarch, Greek Middle Platonist philosopher, biographer, essayist, and priest at the Temple of Apollo

What we achieve inwardly will change outer reality.

Know how to listen and you will profit even from those who talk badly.

Amy Poehler, American actress, comedian, writer, producer, and director

Limit your always and your never.

Michael Porter, American academic, author

The essence of strategy is choosing what not to do.

General Colin Powell, An American Politician, former US Secretary of State, and retired four-star general of the US Army

Leadership is solving problems. The day soldiers stop bringing you their problems is the day you have stopped leading them. They have either lost confidence that you can help or concluded you do not care. Either case is a failure of leadership.

Great leaders are almost always great simplifiers, who can cut through argument, debate, and doubt to offer a solution everybody can understand.

There are no secrets to success. It is the result of preparation, hard work, and learning from failure.

Strategy equals execution.

The most important thing I learned is that soldiers watch what their leaders do. You can give them classes and lecture them forever, but it is your personal example they will follow.

Steve Prefontaine, American long-distance runner, record setter

> Don't be afraid to give up the good and go for the great.

> To give anything less than your best is to sacrifice the gift.

Marcel Proust, French novelist, critic, and essayist

> We must never be afraid to go too far, for success lies just beyond.

Pierre-Joseph Proudhon, French politician and the founder of mutualist philosophy

> When deeds speak, words are nothing.

Nido Qubein, American Lebanese-Jordanian businessman and motivational speaker

> Your present circumstances don't determine where you can go; they merely determine where you start.

Queen Elizabeth II, Queen of the United Kingdom and the other Commonwealth realms (1952 - present)

> I know of no single formula for success. But over the years I have
> observed that some attributes of leadership are universal and are often about finding ways of encouraging people to combine their efforts, their talents, their insights, their enthusiasm and their inspiration to work together.

Ayn Rand, Russian-American writer and philosopher
Throughout the centuries there were men who took the first steps, down new roads, armed with nothing but their own vision.

The ladder of success is best climbed by stepping on the rungs of opportunity.

A creative man is motivated by the desire to achieve, not the desire to beat others.

Jag Randhawa, Author and speaker
All employees have an innate desire to contribute to something bigger than themselves.

Jeanette Rankin, American politician and women's rights advocate
You take people as far as they will go, not as far as you would like them to go.

Tom Rath, American consultant and author
What great leaders have in common is that each truly knows his or her strengths - and can call on the right strength at the right time.

If you spend your life trying to be good at everything, you will never be great at anything.

Sam Rayburn, Former American politician
You cannot be a leader, and ask other people to follow you, unless you know how to follow, too.

President Ronald Reagan, US President (1981-1989)

> The greatest leader is not necessarily the one who does the greatest things. He is the one that gets the people to do the greatest things.

> There are no constraints on the human mind, no walls around the human spirit, no barriers to our progress except those we ourselves erect.

> The future doesn't belong to the fainthearted; it belongs to the brave.

Jeremy Renner, American actor, musician and songwriter

> I live my life through freak. If I'm afraid of it, I'll do it just so I'm not afraid of it anymore.

Jerry Rice, American former professional football player, National Football League Hall of Fame inductee

> I think the thing about that was I was always willing to work; I was not the fastest player or the biggest player but I was determined to be the best football player I could be on the football field and I think I was able to accomplish that through hard work.

Edward Rickenbacker, American fighter ace in World War I and Medal of Honor recipient

> I can give you a six-word formula for success: Think things through--then follow through.

Pat Riley, American professional basketball executive and a former coach and player in the National Basketball Association

> If you have a positive attitude and constantly strive to give your best effort, eventually you will overcome your immediate problems and find you are ready for greater challenges.

Tony Robbins, American author, public speaker, life coach, and philanthropist

> When you raise your standards, your shoulds become your musts.

> We all get what we tolerate.

> Trade your expectation for appreciation and the world changes instantly.

> The path to success is to take massive, determined actions.

> Complexity is the enemy of execution.

> It's your unlimited power to create and to love that can make the biggest difference in the quality of your life.

Jackie Robinson, American professional baseball player, first African American to play in Major League Baseball in the modern era

> Life is not a spectator sport.

Sugar Ray Robinson, American professional boxer, World Champion, inductee International Boxing Hall of Fame

> To be a champ, you have to believe in yourself when no one else will.

John D. Rockefeller, American business magnate and philanthropist

> Don't blame the marketing department. The buck stops with the chief executive.

> The secret of success is to do the common thing uncommonly well.

Anita Roddick, British businesswoman, human rights activist and environmental campaigner

> What I have learned is that people become motivated when you guide them to the source of their own power and when you make heroes out of employees who personify what you want to see in the organization.

Will Rogers, American stage and film actor, vaudeville performer, cowboy, humorist, newspaper columnist, and social commentator

> Even if you're on the right track, you'll get run over if you just sit there. Will Rogers

> Good judgement comes from experience, and a lot of that comes from bad judgement.

Jim Rohn, American entrepreneur, author and motivational speaker

The challenge of leadership is to be strong, but not rude; be kind, but not weak; be bold, but not bully; be thoughtful, but not lazy; be humble, but not timid; be proud, but not arrogant; have humor, but without folly.

A good objective of leadership is to help those who are doing poorly to do well and to help those who are doing well to do even better.

Don't wish it was easier, wish you were better. Don't wish for less problems, wish for more skills. Don't wish for less challenges, wish for more wisdom. The major value in life is not what you get. The major value in life is what you become. Success is not to be pursued; it is to be attracted by the person you become.

A formal education will make you a living; self-education will make you a fortune.

Things don't get better until you get better.

Eleanor Roosevelt, First Lady of the United States (1933-1945)

To handle yourself, use your head; to handle others, use your heart.

It takes as much energy to wish as it does to plan.

You gain strength, courage and confidence by every experience in which you really stop to look fear in the face. You must do the thing you think you cannot do.

President Franklin D. Roosevelt, US President (1933-1945)

Go for the moon. If you don't get it, you'll still be heading for a star. Happiness lies to in the mere possession of money; it lies in the joy of achievement, in the thrill of the creative effort.

President Theodore Roosevelt, US President (1901-1909)

People ask the difference between a leader and a boss. The leader leads, and the boss drives.

Keep your eyes on the stars and your feet on the ground.

The most important single ingredient in the formula of success is knowing how to get along with people.

Believe you can and you're halfway there.

It is not the critic who counts; not the man who points out how the strong man stumbles, or where the doer of deeds could have done them better. The credit belongs to the man who is actually in the arena, whose face is marred by dust and sweat and blood; who strives valiantly; who errs, who comes short again and again, because there is no effort without error and shortcoming; but who does actually strive to do the deeds; who knows great enthusiasms, the great devotions; who spends himself in a worthy cause; who at the best knows in the end the triumph of high achievement, and who at the worst, if he fails, at least fails while daring greatly, so that his place shall never be with those cold and timid souls who neither know victory nor defeat. — President Theodore Roosevelt

Do all that you can with all you have, wherever you are.

Courtesy is as much a mark of a gentleman as courage.

The best executive is the one who has sense enough to pick good men to do what he wants done, and self-restraint to keep from meddling with them while they do it.

It is hard to fail, but it is worse never to have tried to succeed.

Diana Ross, American singer, actress, and record producer

Instead of looking at the past, I put myself ahead 20 years and try to look at what I need to do now in order to get there then.

Joseph Rost, Distinguished scholar in leadership studies

In leadership writ large, mutually agreed upon purposes help people achieve consensus, assume responsibility, work for the common good, and build community.

J. K. Rowling, British author, film producer, television producer, screenwriter, and philanthropist

It takes a great deal of courage to stand up to your enemies, but even more to stand up to your friends.

Deep Roy, (Gurdeep Roy) Kenyan-born Indian-American actor, stuntman and puppeteer

Inspiration comes from within yourself. One has to be positive. When you're positive, good things happen.

Arthur Rubinstein, Polish American classical pianist

I have found that if you love life, life will love you back.

Wilma Rudolph, American sprinter, Olympic champion

Never underestimate the power of dreams and the influence of the human spirit. We are all the same in this notion: The potential for greatness lives within each of us.

Babe Ruth, George Herman Ruth, American professional baseball player
Every strike brings me closer to the next home run.

Yesterday's home runs don't win today's games.

It's hard to beat a person who never gives up.

Mark Sanborn, Author, professional speaker, and entrepreneur
The test of leadership is, is anything or anyone better because of you?

Sheryl Sandberg, American technology executive, author, and billionaire
Leadership is about making others better as a result of your presence and making sure that impact lasts in your absence.

In the future, there will be no female leaders. There will just be leaders.

Motivation comes from working on things we care about.

Brandon Sanderson, American fantasy and science fiction writer
The mark of a great man is one who knows when to set aside the important things in order to accomplish the vital ones.

Vidal Sasson, British-American hairstylist,
businessman, and philanthropist
> The only place where success comes before work is
> in the dictionary.

Ryunosuke Satoro, Japanese writer
> Individually, we are one drop. Together, we are an
> ocean.

George Savile, 1st Marquees of Halifax, English
statesman, writer, and politician
> A man who is a master of patience is a master of
> everything else.

Gayle Sayers, American former professional football
player
> I learned that if you want to make it bad enough,
> no matter how bad it is, you can make it.

Arthur Schopenhauer, German philosopher
> Every truth passes through three stages before it is
> recognized. In the first, it is ridiculed. In the
> second, it is opposed. In the third, it is regarded as
> self-evident.

Dr. Robert Schuller, American Christian televangelist,
pastor, motivational speaker, and author
> Tough times never last, but tough people do.

> What great thing would you attempt if you know
> you could not fail?

Howard Schultz, American businessman, author, and philanthropist

Success is empty if you arrive at the finish line alone. The best reward is to get there surrounded by winners.

Charles M. Schwab, American steel magnate

A man can succeed at almost anything for which he has unlimited enthusiasm.

I consider my ability to arouse enthusiasm among men the greatest asset I possess. The way to develop the best that is in a man is by appreciation and encouragement.

General Norman Schwarzkopf, 4 star United States Army General

The truth of the matter is that you always know the right thing to do. The hard part is doing it.

Albert Schweitzer, Theologian, organist, writer, humanitarian, philosopher, and physician

I don't know what your destiny will be, but one thing I know: The only ones among you who will be truly happy are those who have sought and found how to serve.

Seneca, Roman Stoic philosopher, statesman, dramatist

If a man knows not to which port he sails, no wind is favorable.

It is a rough road that leads to the heights of greatness.

The pressure of adversity does not affect the mind of the brave man. It is more powerful than external circumstances.

Most powerful is he who has himself in his own power.

He who has great power should use it lightly.

We suffer more in imagination than in reality.

The bravest sight in the world is to see a great man struggling against adversity.

No man was ever wise by chance.

Associate with people who are likely to improve you.

St Catherine of Siena, laywoman associated with the Dominican Order, was a mystic, activist, and author
Nothing great was ever done without much enduring.

William Shakespeare, English poet, playwright, and actor
It is not in the stars to hold our destiny, but in ourselves.

Readied and waiting. The readiness is all.

How poor are they that have not patience! What wound did ever heal but by degrees?

This above all: to thine own self be true.

Our doubts are traitors and make us lose the good we oft might win by fearing to attempt.

Be not afraid of greatness; some are born great, some achieve greatness, and others have greatness thrust upon them.

Robin S. Sharma, Canadian Author and speaker
Leadership is not about a title or a designation. It's about impact, influence, and inspiration.

Ideation without execution is delusion.

George Bernard Shaw, Irish playwright, critic, polemicist and political activist
The reasonable man adapts itself to the world; the unreasonable one persists in trying to adapt the world to himself. Therefore, all progress depends on the unreasonable man.

People are always blaming their circumstances for what they are. I don't believe in circumstances. The people who get on in this world are the people who get up and look for the circumstances they want and if they can't find them make them.

Life isn't about finding yourself. Life is about creating yourself.

John A. Shedd, American author and professor
A ship in harbor is safe, but that is not what ships are built for.

James R. Sherman, Ph. D., Author
Though no one can go back and make a brand new start, anyone can start from now and make a brand new ending.

Jensen Siaw, Asia's Bilingual Motivational Speaker on Sales Motivation, Leadership Development & Team Performance
Don't wait until you are ready to take action, take action to be ready.

Frank Sinatra, American singer, actor and producer
Don't hide your scars, they make you who you are.

Simon Sinek, Author and motivational speaker
A star wants to see himself rise to the top. A leader wants to see those around him rise to the top.

A boss has the title, a leader has the people.

The leaders who get the most out of their people are the leaders who care most about their people.

Unless you give motivated people something to believe in, something bigger than their job to work toward, they will motivate themselves to find a new job and you'll be stuck with whoever's left.

If you hire people just because they can do a job, they'll work for your money. But if you hire people who believe what you believe, they'll work for you with blood and sweat and tears.

People don't buy what you do, they buy why you do it.

When people are financially invested, they want a return. When people are emotionally invested, they want to contribute.

Samuel Smiles, Scottish author and government reformer
We learn wisdom from failure much more than from success; we often discover what will do, by finding out what will not do; and probably he who never made a mistake never made a discovery.

Socrates, classical Greek philosopher credited as one of the founders of Western philosophy
The way to gain a good reputation Is to endeavor to be what you desire to appear.

Falling down is not a failure. Failure comes when you stay where you have fallen.

Thomas Sowell, Thomas Sowell, American economist and social theorist
People who enjoy meetings should not be in charge of anything.

Sylvester Stallone, American actor, director, screenwriter, and producer
Winners are the ones who really listen to the truth of their heart.

Roger Staubach, American former professional football player, National Football League Hall of Fame Inductee
There are no traffic jams along the extra mile.

Gloria Steinem, American feminist, journalist, and social political activist
Without leaps of imagination, or dreaming, we lose the excitement of possibilities. Dreaming, after all, is a form of planning.

Laurence Sterne, Anglo-Irish novelist and an Anglican clergyman
Respect for ourselves guides our morals, respect for others guides our manners.

Sybil F. Stershic, Author, speaker, facilitator
The way your employees feel is the way your customers will feel. And if your employees don't feel valued, neither will your customers.

Robert Louis Stevenson, Scottish novelist and travel writer
Keep your fears to yourself but share your courage with others.

Don't judge each day by the harvest you reap, but by the seeds you plant.

Biz Stone, American entrepreneur
Timing, perseverance, and 10 years of trying will eventually make you look like an overnight success.

W. Clement Stone, businessman, philanthropist and author
Definiteness of purpose is the starting point of all achievement.

Be careful the environment you choose, for it will shape you; be careful the friends you choose, for you will be like them.

Neil Strauss, American author, journalist and ghostwriter
Great things never come from comfort zones.

Tracy Streckenbach, Businessperson
Culture is about performance, and making people feel good about how they contribute to the whole.

Taylor Swift, American singer-songwriter
Giving up doesn't always mean you're weak. Sometimes you're just strong enough to let go.

Charles Swindoll, Evangelical Christian pastor, author, educator, and radio preacher
Life is 10% what happens to you and 90% how you react to it.

Herbert Bayard Swope, U.S. editor, Pulitzer Prize winning journalist

> I can't give you a surefire formula for success, but I can give you a formula for failure: try to please everybody all the time.

Publilius Syrus, Latin writer

> Anyone can hold the helm when the sea is calm.

President William Howard Taft, US President (1909-1913)

> Don't write so that you can be understood, write so that you can't be misunderstood.

Margaret Thatcher, British stateswoman, Prime Minister of the United Kingdom (1979-1990)

> I do not know anyone who has gotten to the top without hard work. That is the recipe. It will not always get you to the top but should get you pretty near.

> Don't follow the crowd, let the crowd follow you.

Eric Thomas, Ph. D., American motivational speaker, author and minister

> Things change for the better when we take responsibility for our own thoughts, decisions and actions.

> When you want to succeed as bad as you want to breathe, then you'll be successful.

Only those who risk going too far can possibly find out how far one can go.

Henry David Thoreau, American essayist, poet, and philosopher
Go confidently in the direction of your dreams. Live the live you've imagined.

It is not what you look at that matters, it's what you see.

A man is rich in proportion to the number of things he can afford to let alone.

You must not only aim right but draw the bow with all your might.

I also have in mind that seemingly wealthy, but most terribly impoverished class of all, who have accumulated dross, but know not how to use it, or get rid of it, and thus have forged their own golden or silver fetters.

Thucydides, Athenian historian and general
The bravest are surely those who have the clearest vision of what is before them, glory and danger alike, and yet notwithstanding, go out and meet it.

Rodd Thunderheart, Author
A man is only as good as his words are.

Leo Tolstoy, Russian writer
Everyone thinks of changing the world, but no one thinks of changing himself.

Robert Townsend, American actor, director, comedian, and writer
A leader is not an administrator who loves to run others, but someone who carries water for his people so that they can get on with their jobs.

Brian Tracy, Canadian-American motivational public speaker and self-development author
Become the kind of leader that other people would follow voluntarily; even if you had no title or position.

Leaders think and talk about the solutions. Followers think and talk about the problems.

Winners make a habit of manufacturing their own positive expectations in advance of the event.

President Harry S. Truman, US President (1945-1953)
America was not built on fear. America was built on courage, on imagination, and an unbeatable determination to do the job at hand.

President Donald J. Trump, US President (2017 - present)
Leaders, true leaders, take responsibility for the success of the team, and understand that they must also take responsibility for the failure.

No dream is too big. No challenge is too great. Nothing we want for our future is beyond our reach.

In the end, you're measured not by how much you undertake but by what you finally accomplish.

What separates the winners from the losers is how a person reacts to each new twist of fate.

Remember, there's no such thing as an unrealistic goal—just unrealistic time frames.

As long as you're going to be thinking anyway, think big.

Criticism is easier to take when you realize that the only people who aren't criticized are those who don't take risks.

Harriet Tubman, American abolitionist and political activist
Every great dream begins with a dreamer. Always remember, you have within you the strength, the patience and the passion to reach for the stars and to change the world.

Desmond Tutu, South African Anglican cleric and theologian, anti-apartheid and human rights activist
Don't raise your voice. Improve your argument.

Mark Twain, Samuel Langhorne Clemens, known by his pen name Mark Twain, was an American writer, humorist, entrepreneur, publisher, and lecturer

The two most important days in your life are the day you are born and the day you find out why.

I am an old man and have known a great many troubles, but most of them never happened.

The secret of getting ahead is getting started.

Do not argue with an idiot. He will drag you down to his level and beat you with experience.

It is better to keep your mouth closed and let people think you are a fool than to open it and remove all doubt.

Whenever you find yourself on the side of the majority, it is time to pause and reflect.

Keep away from people who try to belittle your ambitions. Small people always do that, but the really great make you feel that you, too, can become great.

Twenty years from now you will be more disappointed by the things you didn't' do than by the ones you did do, so throw off the bow lines, sail away from safe harbor, catch the Tradewinds in your sails. Explore. Dream. Discover.

President John Tyler, US President (1841-1845)
Popularity, I have always thought, may aptly be compared to a coquette - the more you woo her, the more apt is she to elude your embrace.

Mike Tyson, American former professional boxer, undisputed heavyweight champion
Everyone has a plan until they get punched in the mouth.

Neil deGrasse Tyson, American astrophysicist, author, and science communicator
We live in the kind of society where, in almost all cases, hard work is rewarded.

Lao Tzu, Ancient Chinese philosopher and writer
If you realize that all things change, there is nothing you will try to hold on to. If you are not afraid of dying, there is nothing you cannot achieve.

A leader is best when people barely know he exists. When his work is done, his aim fulfilled, they will all say: We did it ourselves.
Care about what other people think and you'll always be their prisoner.

I have three precious things which I hold fast and prize. The first is gentleness; the second is frugality; the third is humility, which keeps me from putting myself before others. Be gentle and you can be bold; be frugal and you can be liberal; avoid putting yourself before others and you can become a leader among men.

Sun Tzu, Chinese general, military strategist, writer and philosopher
>In the midst of chaos, there's is also opportunity.

>Opportunities multiply as they are seized.

President Martin Van Buren, US President (1837-1841)
>It is easier to do a job right than to explain why you didn't.

>Most men are not scolded out of their opinion.

Gary Vaynerchuck, Belarusian-American entrepreneur, author, speaker, and Internet personality
>When it all comes down to it, nothing trumps execution.

Virgil, (Publius Vergilius Maro) Ancient Roman poet of the Augustan period
>They can conquer who believe they can.

Johann Wolfgang von Goethe, German writer and statesman
>A great person attracts great people and knows how to hold them together.

>Knowing is not enough; we must apply. Wishing is not enough; we must do.

>What is not started will never get finished.

Treat people as if they were what they ought to be, and you help them become what they are capable of being.

Kurt Vonnegut, American writer
We are what we pretend to be, so we must be careful about what we pretend to be.

Dita Von Teese, American vedette, burlesque dancer, model, costume designer, entrepreneur, singer, and actress
You can be the ripest, juiciest peach in the world and there are still going to be some people who hate peaches.

Marilyn Vos Savant, American magazine columnist, author, lecturer, and playwright
Being defeated is often a temporary condition. Giving up is what makes it permanent.

Dennis Waitley, American motivational speaker, writer and consultant
The winners in life think constantly in terms of I can, I will, I am. Losers, on the other hand, concentrated their waking thoughts on what they should have or would have done, or what they can't do.

Alice Walker, American novelist, short story writer, poet, and social activist
The most common way people give up their power is by thinking they don't have any.

Neal Donald Walsch, American author
Life begins at the end of your comfort zone.

Bill Walton, American former basketball player,
television sportscaster, and Basketball Hall of Fame
inductee
Success at the highest level comes down to one
question: Can you decide that your happiness can
come from someone else's success?

Sam Walton, American businessman, entrepreneur,
founder of Walmart
There is only one boss. The customer. And he can
fire everybody in the company, from the chairman
on down, simply by spending his money
somewhere else.

Outstanding leaders go out of their way to boost
the self-confidence of their personnel. If people
believe in themselves, it's amazing what they can
accomplish.

William Arthur Ward, Writer
When we seek to discover the best in others, we
somehow bring out the best in ourselves.

The mediocre teacher tells. The good teacher
explains. The superior teacher demonstrates. The
great teacher inspires.

Booker T. Washington, American educator, author, orator, and adviser to multiple presidents of the United States

If you want to lift yourself up, lift up someone else.

President George Washington, US President (1789-1797)

Require nothing unreasonable of your officers and men but see that whatever is required be punctually complied with. Reward and punish every man according to his merit, without partiality or prejudice; hear his complaints; if well founded, redress them; if otherwise, discourage them, in order to prevent frivolous ones. Discourage vice in every shape, and impress upon the mind of every man, from the first to the lowest, the importance of the cause, and what it is they are contending for.

Remember that it is the actions, and not the commission, that make the officer, and that there is more expected from him, than the title.

99% of failures come from people who make excuses.

Happiness depends more upon the internal frame of a person's own mind, than on the externals in the world.

Martha Washington, First Lady of the United States (1789-1797)

The greater part of our misery or unhappiness is determined not by our circumstance, but by our disposition.

Thomas J. Watson, American businessman, former chairman and CEO of IBM

As of this second, quit doing less than excellent work.

Dave Weinbaum, Writer, comedian, radio host

Those who let things happen usually lose to those who make things happen.

Jack Welch, American business executive, chemical engineer, and writer

People have to trust you. You have to build in trust for people.

Good business leaders create a vision, articulate the vision, passionately own the vision, and relentlessly drive it to completion.

Before you are a leader, success is all about growing yourself. When you become a leader, success is all about growing others.

Change before you have to.

Edith Wharton, American novelist, short story writer, playwright, and designer
There are two ways of spreading light: to be the candle or the mirror that reflects it.

Margaret J. Wheatley, American writer and management consultant
Leadership is a series of behaviors rather than a role for heroes.

The things we fear most in organizations--fluctuations, disturbances, imbalances--are the primary sources of creativity.

Walt Whitman, American poet, essayist, and journalist
Keep your face always toward the sunshine and shadows will fall behind you.

We convince by our presence. — Walt Whitman

Frank Wilczek, American theoretical physicist, mathematician and a Nobel laureate
If you don't make mistakes, you're not working on hard enough problems. And that's a big mistake.

Oscar Wilde, Irish poet and playwright
Yes, I am a dreamer. For a dreamer is one who can find his way by moonlight and see the dawn before the rest of the world.

Michael K. Williams, American actor
The most successful people reach the top not because they are free of limitations, but because they act in spite of their limitations.

Robin Williams, American actor and comedian
No matter what people tell you, words and ideas can change the world.

Roger Williams, Puritan minister, theologian, and author
The greatest crime in the world is not developing your potential. When you do what you do best, you are helping not only yourself but the world.

Serena Williams, American professional tennis player and former world No. 1 in women's single tennis
A champion is defined not by their wins, but by how they recover when they fail.

Ted Williams, American professional baseball player and manager
Just keep going. Everybody gets better if they keep at it.

Marianne Williamson, American author, spiritual leader, politician, and activist
Our deepest fear is that we are powerful beyond measure.

Jocko Willink, Retired officer of the US Navy, author, podcaster

Leadership requires belief in the mission and unyielding perseverance to achieve victory.

Leading people is the most challenging and, therefore, the most gratifying undertaking of all human endeavors.

President Woodrow Wilson, US President (1913-1921)

I not only use all the brains that I have, but all that I can borrow.

One cool judgment is worth a thousand hasty counsels. The thing to do is to supply light and not heat.

You are not here merely to make a living. You are here in order to enable the world to live more amply, with greater vision, with a finer spirit of hope and achievement. You are here to enrich the world, and you impoverish yourself if you forget the errand.

Life does not consist in thinking; it consists in acting.

The man who is swimming against the stream knows the strength of it.

The ear of the leader must ring with the voices of the people.

If you want to make enemies, try to change something.

Oprah Winfrey, American media executive, actress, talk show host, television producer, and philanthropist
You know when you are on the road to success if you would do your job and not be paid for it.

There is no such thing as failure. Failure is just life trying to move us in another direction.

If you look at what you have in life, you'll always have more.

Reese Witherspoon, American actress, producer, and entrepreneur
With the right kind of coaching and determination you can accomplish anything.

John Wooden, American basketball player and head coach at the University of California, Los Angeles
A coach is someone who can give correction without causing resentment.

Success comes from knowing that you did your best to become the best that you are capable of becoming.

Don't measure yourself by what you have accomplished, but by what you should have accomplished with your ability.

Do not let what you cannot do interfere with what you can do.

Things work out best for those who make the best of how things work out.

Make each day your masterpiece

If you don't have time to do it right, when will you have time to do it over?

Failure is not fatal, but failure to change might be.

Talent is God given. Be humble. Fame is man-given. Be grateful. Conceit is self-given. Be careful.

Just try to be the best you can be; never cease trying to be the best you can be. That's in your power.

You can't let praise or criticism get to you. It's a weakness to get caught up in either one.

Be more concerned with your character than your reputation, because your character is what you really are, while your reputation is merely what others think you are.

Success is never final; failure is never fatal. It's courage that counts.

Success is peace of mind, which is a direct result of self-satisfaction in knowing you made the effort to become the best of which you are capable.

Adversity is the state in which man most easily becomes acquainted with himself, being especially free of admirers then.

The best competition I have is against myself to become better.

Whatever you do in life, surround yourself with smart people who'll argue with you.

The main ingredient of stardom is the rest of the team.

Orrin Woodward, American Author and entrepreneur
Average leaders raise the bar on themselves; good leaders raise the bar for others; great leaders inspire others to raise their own bar.

Colin Wright, Author and podcaster
As a general rule, it pays to be confident, helpful and nice.

Frank Lloyd Wright, American architect, interior designer, writer, and educator
I know the price of success: dedication, hard work, and an unremitting devotion to the things you want to see happen.

There is nothing more uncommon than common sense.

Malcolm X, American Muslim minister and human rights activist

The hero journey is inside of you; tear off the veils and open the mystery of yourself.

Yoda, fictional character in the Star Wars universe

Named must your fear be before banish it you can.

Edward Young, English poet, critic, philosopher and theologian

Too low they build, who build beneath the stars.

Sir Mark A. Young, British administrator, former Governor of Hong Kong

Be who you are and say what you feel, because those who mind don't matter and those who matter don't mind.

John Zenger, German printer and journalist (1697-1746)

Great leaders are not defined by the absence of weakness, but rather by the presence of clear strengths.

Zig Ziglar, American author, salesman, and motivational speaker

The real opportunity for success lies within the person and not in the job.

You can have everything in life you want, if you will just help other people get what they want.

What you get by achieving your goals is not as important as what you come by achieving your goals.

If you can dream it, you can achieve it.

You were born to win, but to be a winner, you must plan to win, prepare to win, and expect to win.

People often say that motivation doesn't last. Well, neither does bathing - that's why we recommend it daily.

Do not be distracted by criticism. Remember the only taste of success some people get is to take a bite out of you.

One of the main reasons people fail to reach their full potential is because they are unwilling to risk anything.

What you get by achieving your goals is not as important as what you come by achieving your goals.

Conclusion

Thank you again for downloading 1001 Quotes for Great Leaders: Powerful Leadership Quotes for Inspiration, Motivation and Perspective. I hope you had a chance to download the Leader's guide to inspire your own thoughts about your great leadership.

If you enjoyed the book, please leave a review. I appreciate your support.

I wish you the very best as you continue on your path to great leadership!

A

B

275

Printed in Great Britain
by Amazon